The Training Camp™ Guide to

SPORTS PARENTING:
Encouraging Your Kids On and Off the Field

The Training Camp™ Guide to

SPORTS PARENTING:
Encouraging Your Kids On and Off the Field

Rick Wolff

Byron Preiss Multimedia
Company, Inc.

New York

A Training Camp™ Book

Pocket Books

New York London Toronto

Sydney Tokyo Singapore

An original publication of POCKET BOOKS

POCKET BOOKS, a division of Simon & Schuster Inc.
1230 Avenue of the Americas, New York, NY 10020

Copyright ©1998 Genesis Direct, Inc. All rights reserved.
A Training Camp™ Book, published by Byron Preiss Multimedia Company, Inc.

Byron Preiss Multimedia Company, Inc.
24 West 25th Street
New York, New York 10010
The Training Camp World Wide Web Site address is **www.trainingcamp.com**
The Byron Preiss Multimedia World Wide Web Site Address is **www.byronpreiss.com**

ISBN 0-671-01198-7
First Pocket Books paperback printing September 1998
10 9 8 7 6 5 4 3 2 1

Editor: Ruth Ashby
Cover design: Steven Jablonoski
Interior design: Eric Baker Associates

Printed in the U.S.A.

For Trish . . . who's the real coach

Putting together a book is never a simple process, and to that end, I'd be remiss if I didn't take the time to honor those people who made this book into a reality. To that end, my sincere thanks to Stephen Samuels, who had the vision to take this project from a simple idea to a finished book; to my editor, Ruth Ashby, who oversaw the project from beginning to end and did so with grace and flair; to Byron Preiss and his fine editorial staff, and to Steve Young and Stefani Wanicur, for their kind assistance and support on the book.

CONTENTS

Foreword

Butch and his father, George L. Seewagen, in 1959.

I have been an athlete all of my life. When I was still in my crib, my mom and dad began bouncing balloons and rolling balls with me. Dad, a legendary New York City high school athlete and five-letter man, was drafted by the New York Yankees when Ruth and Gehrig were still playing. He chose college instead, where he took up tennis in his senior year. From then on, tennis consumed him. For nearly fifty years, he coached the St. John's University tennis team and taught physical education in the New York City school system.

So Dad knew a thing or two about teaching sports to kids.

By the age of five, I was smacking tennis balls around the courts, the parks, the driveway, the living room—anywhere and anytime I could. I have an old home movie that shows an elegant backhand for a pretty small guy.

What stuck with me most from those early days, what I remember with some awe, was how Dad intuitively knew that there was fun to be had on the playing fields. Never once did he have to make me practice. I was never over-coached; instead, we played lots of tournaments. Dad always said that relentless drills were like playing the piano scales all day and never getting a chance to play a song.

As a result, I never thought of tennis as work. I remember watching Dad play a match, and eagerly waiting my turn to play with him. He was always supportive and positive. He was also wise: when I was about eight years old, I lost a game and threw a fit—and my racquet—on the court. Dad, always the gentleman and impeccably dressed in long white tennis flannels, was appalled. (This was the man who made us polish our tennis shoes before every match.) Soon after, Dad and I were playing a doubles game. In the middle of a point, he flubbed a shot and began to yell, flinging his racquet as far as he could and stomping his foot. I froze in embarrassment and disbelief. After a beat, he turned to me and said simply, "That is what you look like."

I never had an on-court tantrum again.

When he taught, Dad avoided what most teaching pros still do—constantly drilling and barking out instructions. Instead, Dad would take an absolute beginner and have them rally over the net immediately. When I asked him why he didn't just hit a basket of balls to the kid, he said firmly, "That's not tennis. Tennis is the rally. That's the fun of the game; that's what gives you a sense of the sport. Not rote drilling the perfect forehand."

The essence of the sport. The fun of the sport. That's what Dad believed in, that's how I teach kids, and that's what The Training Camp is all about.

The Training Camp Guide to Sports Parenting: Encouraging Your Kids On and Off the Field is the first of a series of Training Camp books on the world of sports and kids. A companion guide to The Training Camp videos, the www.trainingcamp.com website, and The Training Camp catalog, *Sports Parenting* targets parents who want to make their children's sports experiences a better and more successful time for all members of the family, not just the kids.

I have trained over 20,000 kids on basic sports skills and attitudes and I'm always learning something new that I can pass on to the next generation of athletes and coaches. I'd love to hear your best anecdotes and tips. Send them to me at The Training Camp, 100 Plaza Drive, Secaucus, New Jersey 07094, or e-mail me at butchs@genesisdirect.com.

Welcome to The Training Camp!

Butch Seewagen
Head Coach, The Training Camp

Butch Seewagen has devoted his life to athletics, education and chidren. After a successful career as a world-class tennis star, Butch embarked on a distinguished twenty-five-year career as coach and educator.

INTRODUCTION
A ROAD MAP THROUGH SPORTS FOR KIDS

Wherever I give speaking engagements on kids and sports, anxious parents pepper me with questions about their kids:

→ "At what age should my child start playing organized sports? Is six years old too early . . . or too late?"

→ "My nine-year-old didn't make the travel team in soccer, and she's absolutely devastated. She feels like quitting playing the game altogether. What should I say to her?"

→ "My son's baseball coach is loud and verbally abusive to the kids. I feel like saying something to him, but as a parent I'm not sure I ought to interfere. What should I do?"

→ "People tell us all the time that our daughter has a real talent for ice-skating. She is pretty good at it and she just loves it. We've been thinking about getting her into a top-notch touring program, but that means taking her out of school and away from her friends. How old is she? Well, she's ten . . ."

Travel team?

Top-notch touring program?

Whatever happened to the Good Old Days, when playing sports meant a bunch of kids playing pickup baseball, kickball, basketball, or football at a local playground or park? When kids managed to choose up sides, decide on rules, and play for hours all on their own—without uniforms, officials, or any kind of grown-up guidance? When did it all get so complicated?

Today, more kids are playing more kinds of sports than ever before.

Many of today's parents, faced with the complexity of their kids' involvement with sports, are struck by the contrast with their own childhood experience, when they just went out and played on their own, inventing games and sports to suit their whims, resources, and the local terrain. After all, a couple of grown-ups named Naismith and Doubleday may have been responsible for the official rules of basketball and baseball, but it was a kid who came up with stoopball, stickball, and kick-the-can.

Well, the Good Old Days are exactly that—old. And they're not coming back. Today, when it comes to our kids' involvement in sports, whether on a team or in an individual sport, the coaching and parenting landscape has changed dramatically. But that doesn't mean today's kids can't have their own Good Old Days. Most community sports organizations do a great job volunteering their time and working with our kids to have fun playing sports.

Sure it's a lot more complicated today. The list of questions, problems, and potential traps seems endless. Parents want answers and solutions, and who can blame them? After all, moms and dads just want to make sure they do what's best for their kids.

A ball, a bat, a kid, and a sunny day—that's what baseball is all about. Isn't it?

But sadly, in these highly pressurized, highly demanding times, it's easy to lose track of the best thing that sports can provide a child: good, healthy fun.

Now, when I say sports, I mean all sorts of activities you might not automatically think of, including team sports like soccer, baseball, and basketball; individual sports like tennis, golf, swimming, and gymnastics; and recreational sports like biking, hiking and jogging. It doesn't matter what sporting activity your child takes an interest in. What *does* matter is that youngsters enjoy mastering athletic skills, feel good about themselves, and take pride in their accomplishments.

Whether it's playing for the league championship or just throwing a Frisbee around with a few buddies, sports is—and always has been—about having fun. That's what it's supposed to be about.

I never set out to become a national youth sports advocate for kids and parents. All I wanted, like millions of other parents in this country and around the world, was to find out how my own kids could best enjoy sports.

In the early 1990s, my kids were just old enough to sign up for our community's youth league teams. Naturally I'd heard all the horror stories about win-at-all-costs Little League coaches, pushy parents whose demand for excellence ruins their kid's love of the game, and amateur sports' boards governing groups who seem to have stricken the word "fun" from their vocabulary. Like every other parent, I needed a little guidance.

The Training Camp™ Philosophy

It's simple. Kids who have positive sports experiences are more likely to enjoy higher self-esteem, be more self-motivated, and have a stronger sense of teamwork and a better conception of true sportsmanship—on the field and throughout their lives. And when parents are involved in kids' sports activities, the rewards are even greater . . . *for the whole family.*

The Training Camp provides innovative tools that parents can use to help ensure their child's enjoyment of sports. Training Camp books, videos, catalogs and website are filled with practical advice, ideas, and equipment for parents and families at every skill level.

Everything The Training Camp does is designed to help motivate kids—and their parents—to get the most out of sports. The Training Camp philosophy is simple: It's not whether you win or lose . . . it's how you help your kids play the game.

As it happened, for six years I served as the roving performance enhancement coach—in other words, a "sports shrink"—for the Cleveland Indians. As I made my rounds during spring training and throughout the long baseball season, I chatted with a number of major league players, all of whom had played Little League baseball and other youth sports as children.

(*"Sports is about having fun."*)

I'd assumed that most of the major leaguers I spoke with would have lots of warm and fuzzy memories about playing Little League ball. After all, these guys did go on to become huge stars. And in fact most of them did have fond recollections of their childhood playing days. But I was startled to hear other memories that weren't so warm and fuzzy. More than a few of these top athletes said things about Little League baseball that were downright alarming, things like:

→ "No way am I letting my kids play Little League ball. I saw all those crazy moms and dads get involved when I was a kid. No way am I exposing my kids to nuts like that."

→ "I'm not about to trust my kids to some volunteer coach who doesn't know the first thing about working with children. Man, I remember those coaches. They act like yelling and screaming at kids is the way to get the most out of them. No thanks. I'll coach my own. . . ."

→ "A lot of parents forget that the kids are supposed to have fun playing. They worry too much about winning and losing. Who cares if your kid's third-grade team wins the league championship? I mean, they're *third-graders!*"

It's ironic that the very same guys who had once been Little League stars were determined to keep their kids away from Little League. Having seen all the Little League madness firsthand as kids, considering themselves lucky to have gotten through it unscathed, they didn't want to take a chance on spoiling their own kids' sports lives.

The Good News is that the vast majority of parents and coaches (who are usually parents themselves) keep the games in the right frame of mind. The Bad News is that such right-minded parents and coaches are a silent majority. If you want to hear the shrill minority, just head out to any weekend game and check out overwrought dads screaming at referees for making bad calls, stressed-out moms shrieking at their kids, and ulcer-nursing coaches attempting to curse their players on to greater heights.

Sometimes it gets completely out of hand, even in upper-middle-class towns like Chappaqua, NY, where recently a father became so outraged by a bad call during a baseball game that he jumped out of the stands and actually beat up the umpire working the game. It was a game of ten- and eleven-year-olds.

I've seen loud, uncontrolled shouting matches at soccer games—between obsessed moms. I've seen

Parents are their kids' first coaches.

dads climb over the glass at hockey rinks to get in a coach's face. I've seen all sorts of coaches swearing blue streaks in front of their seven- or eight-year-old players.

I've counseled parents who worry not that their kid isn't keeping up with his peer group but that he's not ahead of it. As one mom told me recently, "My son is very upset because he didn't make the All-Star baseball team in our town. Now he thinks he'll never be any good."

I asked the mother how old her son was. When she told me that he was eight, I assured her not to panic just yet—her son's baseball career wasn't quite over.

Still other parents model their behavior after those fabled stories about great athletes whose parents stuck tennis rackets in their cribs, as though a one-year-old is going to have any idea as to what to do with a tennis racket—except, perhaps, drool on it.

Now, I'm not trying to discourage or disparage you with these stories. I just want to reassure you that I've heard them all, lived through them myself, and counseled thousands of parents about them. In fact, the ultimate advice I give moms and dads is this: Before you start worrying about your kids' emotional state, first learn how to control your own emotions. In other words, even though you may be an adult, you have to learn how to act like a grown-up. That's the first step, but it's not as easy as it sounds.

When kids and sports come together, the result is fun

To date, psychological research in the field of youth sports is fairly limited, but several recent studies tend to refute some of the basic beliefs that most youth sports coaches and parents live by. The following results of a *USA Today* poll may surprise you:

→ Some 37 percent of kids ages five to twelve said they wished their parents didn't watch them play their games.

→ Some 41 percent of the kids said that they've awakened in the night worrying about an upcoming game.

→ Some 51 percent observed that they see other kids frequently act like poor sports.

→ Some 71 percent said they wouldn't care if no score were kept in their games.

In another study, more than 90 percent of the children said that they would rather play on a losing team if they could really play in the games than sit on the bench and play infrequently on a team that always wins.

What do these various studies indicate? For starters, they suggest that we parents have to think carefully about what we say and how we behave around our kids. Remember: Your kids pick up quickly on behavioral cues from watching you. That's where it all begins.

For better or for worse, organized sports teams, like this Little League team, are here to stay.

JUST GO OUT AND "HAVE FUN . . ."

Remember to have fun!" That's always the last thing a mom or dad says to a kid before a game. Unfortunately, it's also the first thing a lot of parents forget once the game begins.

Why? For one thing, we sometimes lose sight of the fact that we're looking at our

To find out more about kids and sports, go to www.trainingcamp.com

kids' sports through the filtered lens of our own perspectives. We might forget that we've already grown up, and instinctively compare our own childhood memories with those of our kids. That's a trap you should avoid. Your childhood is over. You can't relive or repair it through your kid. After all, your child has his or her own childhood dreams.

To that end, remember that kids see youth sports in a much brighter, forward-looking light—a prism of optimistic dreams, fun, and success. When you're six or eight or ten years old, you see yourself as the next basketball superstar, World Cup soccer goalie, or Super Bowl quarterback. Indeed, that's what being a kid is all about—chasing dreams.

SHOULD WE PUT AN END TO LITTLE LEAGUE?

"Back when I was a kid, we didn't always have uniforms or leagues or grown-ups umpiring our games—we'd all just show up after school and play our own pickup sandlot games. . . ."

That's a common memory for parents today, who somehow attribute all the evils of youth sports to modern organized leagues. There are two things to remember about this belief:

1. Organized youth sports teams are here to stay. They're deeply woven into the fabric of the American sporting tapestry, and so widespread that there isn't much chance of their disappearing in the near future. So wishing for the unsupervised games of yesteryear is just that—wishful thinking.

At last count, there were close to 3 million kids playing Little League baseball around the world, and that number keeps growing each year. In addition, the explosive popularity of such youth sports as soccer, basketball, ice hockey, and others indicate that more and more kids are playing youth sports than ever before.

2. Convenient as it might be to believe, organized youth sports leagues are NOT the cause of kids' sports woes. Think about it: Is there

something about suiting up for a league game, playing with umpires, or having a coach that's inherently bad for kids?

Of course not. It's when parents, coaches, umpires, and league officials forget that sports leagues are supposed to be about kids that problems arise. When the best interests of the child conflict with the interests of parents and coaches, when the volunteers who run these structured leagues lose sight of the children's top priorities, that's when kids start to suffer, and organized sports leagues get a bad reputation.

$$\left(\begin{array}{l} \textit{"Your kids pick up quickly on behavioral} \\ \textit{clues from watching you."} \end{array} \right)$$

Now I could advise you to avoid any potential problems simply by avoiding popular youth sports leagues. But not only would that make for a very short book, it's not necessary. What I will do is try to give you a better understanding of how your child can enjoy playing organized sports without falling victim to some of the most common traps of kids, parents, and coaches.

In this training guide for parents, I'll make use of the latest research, as well as my own experiences as a coach and parent, to steer you through some of the perplexing situations you and your kids might face when it comes to youth sports. I'll also suggest concrete steps you, as a parent, can take to insure that your child gets the most out of his or her sports experience.

USING THIS BOOK SO THAT EVERYONE WINS

Although this book is a valuable tool for any parent, my focus is on parents whose children are between the ages of four and twelve, and only just learning about youth sports. I'll touch upon a number of key elements that face these developing young athletes and present a number of coaching insights crucial to a child's continuing enjoyment of sports.

None of these insights are etched in stone. Every child is unique. But my experience with professional and top collegiate athletes has revealed a number of issues

common to every child's participation in organized sports. The insight I've gained—from research, interviews and work with top athletes, and my own experiences as a parent—can help you and your kid make the most of youth sports.

Let's get to it.

Sports and kids—a winning combination.

DID YOU KNOW?

Organized youth sports have grown dramatically in the past two decades. For example, the number of kids playing on United States Youth Federation Soccer teams exploded from just over 100,000 in 1975 to more than 2.5 million in 1997.

And the number of girls playing on youth softball teams doubled from 1980 to 1990: a little more than 300,000 girls played in 1980; in 1990, that number jumped to 638,000, and is probably close to a million by now. These numbers show no sign of abating; if anything, everything indicates that they'll continue to grow dramatically in the years to come.

PLAY BALL! INTRODUCING YOUR CHILD TO SPORTS

Hey, Mom and Dad, check out the following comments:

→ "Remember when he was only eight months old? He was swinging a bat in his crib, hitting balls across the room!"

→ "We just dropped her in the pool and she started to swim like a fish. It was uncanny. And to think she was only one year old."

→ "Everybody says he's the most natural athlete they've ever seen. He's just so coordinated for his age. We can't wait to see what he'll do when he turns three."

Sound familiar? Of course it does. In fact, you can pretty much divide the world of parents into two groups: those who make these kinds of statements, and those who have to listen to them. How many parents have never heard boasts about some other child's natural athletic ability or innate genius? After all, what mother or father can resist a brief dream of Olympic glory or World Series heroics when their one-year-old hurdles the dog for the first time?

Sometimes there's even a kernel of truth in such parental boasting. But for the most part, such stories are a simple, understandable expression of pride. There's no harm in them—except, of course, when such stories make other parents worry that their own child isn't yet leaping over bookcases and pushing refrigerators around.

Hearing a fellow parent talk about his kid's prowess, you might think: "Hmm—my kid is four years old, and he hasn't shown the slightest interest in doing anything athletically. He seems content just to sit around, play with his toys, and watch television. Should we start to push him a little into sports?"

Or perhaps you might say to yourself, "Gee, both my wife and I love physical fitness. We've tried to introduce our five-year-old daughter to all the sports we enjoy, but so far she hasn't shown any interest at all. Should we stop even trying?"

Here's the first piece of advice I'll give you: Relax. Remember the overall purpose of playing sports is:

1. To have fun, and
2. To keep physically fit and healthy.

From the moment your child puts her hand on a rubber ball to the day she plays her first basketball game, there's nothing more important for you to remember than those two simple things. Sports, above all, should be about fun and fitness.

FUN—WHAT A CONCEPT!

Classic psychological literature, from Piaget to Adler, stresses the importance of play for children. Play offers a daily opportunity for toddlers (one- to two-year-olds) and preschoolers (three- to five-year-olds) to discover their environment, master basic skills, and develop physical coordination. And the more they play—whether using building blocks, rolling a ball, or trying to conquer the living room sofa—the better off they are.

Fun is an essential part of this progressive exploration and mastery. You know how excited your child gets when you take him to the playground to play on the monkey bars or when you head over to a Discovery Zone.

Every young child is a potential sports star—at least according to his parents!

You can see how much fun he has trying to master even a simple skill, like trying to balance on the edge of the Nerf Pit. And it's obvious that at this age failure is just as much fun as success—whether he's shouting "Look at me!" because he's maintaining his precarious balance or laughing in delight because he's fallen into the pit. It's all play, and it's all fun.

Remember that fun, not performance, is the issue. If it takes your five-year-old a little longer than his friends to learn how to ride a two-wheeler, who cares? Everybody learns at a different pace. What's important is that he set out to ride a bike, eventually mastered the skill, and now enjoys riding with his friends. Could a parent ask for more?

Play enables young children to develop the basic motor skills they will need to succeed in sports.

FIT FOR LIFE

The second benefit of playing sports is that it keeps kids physically fit and healthy. Just as important, kids who develop a "sports habit" at an early age have a good chance of growing up to be physically active adults. Most parents recognize that a kid who enjoys exercise and physical conditioning has a better chance of becoming a fit adult than a kid who develops an early love affair with a lounge chair.

Toddlers and preschoolers need lots of active play—running, jumping, skipping, hopping, rolling, climbing, pushing, pulling—to channel all that energy and develop the physical coordination they'll need for later athletic activities. So give them every opportunity to play in large open spaces where they can really run around—preferably at least once a day. It's far better to have them bouncing on the neighborhood jungle gym than bouncing off the walls. And—you've heard it before but we'll say it again—limit their TV-watching time. Experts have linked an increase in obesity and decline in fitness among American children generally to too much television. Not only is your little couch potato vegetating mentally, she's vegetating physically as well. (Did you know that the metabolic rate of young TV-watchers drops to 16 percent of their normal resting state?) Every minute your four-year-old spends in front of the television, she is spending *not* drawing or looking at books or riding a tricycle or throwing balls for the dog.

LOOK, MA, NO HANDS!

In one respect, the first sport a child discovers is walking. It's challenging, it involves mastering a neuromuscular skill, and there are clear criteria for success (walking) and for nonsuccess (falling over). That sport mastered, the toddler moves on to other skills. Some of them, like running or jumping, can be developed through traditional and informal children's games—tag, hide-and-seek, or monkey-in-the-middle. Your child may be introduced to games such as these through play groups or nursery school or, of course, you—your child's first and favorite playmate.

There are few things toddlers like to do more than throw—food off the table, toys across the room, and balls to you. In another few years, they'll catch, too. Start your pre-Little League practise with big lightweight balls that are easy to pick up and easy to throw.

> *"Kids who develop a sports habit at an early age have a good chance of growing up to be physically active adults."*

You can progress to fleece balls, foam balls, rubber balls, tennis balls and various plastic footballs and baseballs. (Be careful with the foam balls; they can look mighty tasty to a two-year-old.) Children can enjoy throwing balls into makeshift baskets or adjustable basketball nets specially sized for children.

Of all the "grown-up" team sports, soccer is the easiest for preschoolers. This is why the first organized sports children usually join in kindergarten or first grade is a soccer league. You and your child can have lots of fun kicking a ball around the yard or even into a homemade goal.

Another group of skills that preschoolers are ready to master are gymnastic skills—rolling, tumbling, and balancing. You can enroll your kid in a local gymnastics class (gymnastics centers have sprouted all over the United States) or just put a mat in the basement. If you teach your four-year-old to do a somersault (can you still do one yourself?), you'll be surprised how fast she'll progress to cartwheels and backward somersaults.

The younger the child, the more he'll experiment with various activities. Just sit back and let your child explore the environment and develop his own athletic interests. And don't worry about your son or daughter being competitive at these tender ages. When they're first starting out, it's only important that kids feel good about themselves and enjoy the experience of playing sports.

BUT WHAT IF MY CHILD DOESN'T SHOW ANY INTEREST IN SPORTS?

Don't worry. It's not uncommon for a three-or four-year-old to show little interest in traditional athletic activities. Does this mean that your child will never be an athlete, or that he doesn't stand a chance of becoming physically fit?

Of course not. Some young children are more cautious than others or more apprehensive or just more interested in playing with dolls or plastic soldiers than in kicking a ball. To help find the right kind of activities for your child, you might want to make an extra effort to show her how much fun exercise is. Hang out together. Go for walks. Kick a stick or a rock down the road. Climb a tree. Go to the nearest school playground and just start playing. Don't shove your kid toward the jungle gym and say,

To find out more about kids and sports, go to www.trainingcamp.com

On your mark . . . get set . . . go!

¹**fun** \'fən\ *n* [E dial. *fun* to hoax, perh. alter. of **ME** *fonnen*, fr. *fonne* dupe] (1727) **1**: what provides amusement or enjoyment; *specif*: playful often boisterous action or speech.
—*Merriam Webster's Collegiate Dictionary, Tenth Edition.*

"Have fun." Get out there and start climbing yourself! Show your kid how much fun there is to be had. Or you could try a playroom for kids in your neighborhood. Just getting your child to see other kids running around is vital. There's nothing so attractive to a kid as the sight of a bunch of other kids enjoying themselves.

Go outside with your child and have a few simple races. Go through the entire sequence of "on your mark . . . get set . . . go!" and race him to some nearby marker—a tree, fence, or sign. Of course, remember to race as though you were your kid's age, and always make it a point to offer praise and encouragement. You'll find that kids love to race against their Mom or Dad—and win. Don't be surprised if "Let's go race!" becomes part of your daily routine.

Then, whenever you go to work out yourself—aerobic dancing or playing basketball or bike riding—be certain to expose your kid. You don't have to push or prod your child into doing what you're doing; just show him what you enjoy doing and how much fun you have.

Soccer has exploded in popularity during the 1990s. Most kids get their start at five or six years old.

And keep those stories about child athletic prodigies in perspective. Not every major league pitcher could throw a ball when he was two years old. And not every professional golfer could swing a golf club while still in diapers. Very few of today's great athletes can trace their athletic abilities back to the days when they were three, four, or five. For every Tiger Woods or Andre Agassi, there are dozens of top stars who didn't get into sports until much later in their childhood.

THE FIRST "REAL" SPORTS

Many towns and communities offer youth league sports to five- and six-year-olds. For most kids, this will be the first introduction they have to organized sports; they get uniforms, are assigned to a team, have a real coach, and play with their friends. Some get a little nervous with this setup. Oh, they might want to join the team and play because their friends are playing, but still they're reluctant, perhaps because they lack confidence in their abilities or because they're simply shy.

To overcome your child's concerns, you could sit down and explain what happens on these youth league teams, what to expect, and how to have fun. Understanding and adapting to this kind of sporting environment doesn't come naturally to many kids. You have to let them know not just what's expected of them, but how much fun it can be.

And finally, it's important to know that it makes no difference whether your child is a boy or girl. All kids should be encouraged to get into a sport or sports. Naturally, youth sports have traditionally been the domain of dads who have volunteered to be coaches and refs and to administer the youth sports leagues. But with the explosion of women's sports, fueled by Title IX and the success of the WNBA, the opportunities for girls in sports is greater than ever before.

So, whether you're a mom or a dad, the time has come to introduce your kid to the joy and exhilaration of athletics. And along the way, feel free to volunteer your time and energies to help out as a coach, a ref, or an administrator.

Above all, as you go through this book, always remember that it's all about having fun. That's the ultimate key—for moms, for dads, and for kids.

 Sports Parenting Skills Tip

Teach your kid calisthenics by working out with her. That is, set aside some time from your own workout to show your child how to do jumping jacks, leg stretches, sit-ups, leg lifts, and so on. Make the exercises simple enough for her to do. And to make it even more fun, bring along a tape deck and play some toe-tapping golden oldies.

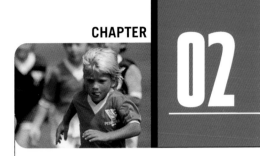

02

A PASSION FOR THE GAME

The single most important thing youth sports can do is to help your child develop a passion for a sport. Any sport.

What do I mean by developing a passion? I mean beginning a love affair with some form of physical activity early in life—a love affair that, with luck, will last a lifetime.

The benefits of this passion for sports don't stop at physical fitness. The ancient Greek philosophy of "a sound body and a sound mind" is as true today as it ever was. A child who plays sports soon learns that playing is both an escape and a release from the grind of everyday life, a mental refreshment as well as a physical challenge. Problems, pressures, and doubts fade away every time a kid steps onto a playing field; it's a break from the built-in anxiety of simply being a kid.

Think about the last time you played a few games of pickup basketball or enjoyed a good tennis match. Regardless of the outcome, no matter how well (or poorly) you played, that hour or so of vigorous exercise was a refreshing tonic, wasn't it?

It's the same for your kids. After spending the whole day sitting in classrooms, they can hardly wait to get outside and cut loose—which is why you often see young kids tearing around at recess, happy to just play and forget about blackboards and textbooks and quizzes.

The "sound body-sound mind" philosophy is still very much at work in our schools today, and it's precisely why elementary schools schedule gym class and recess on a daily basis. Educators know the body-mind connection is vital, and do their best to encourage a love for physical exercise at a young age.

"Develop a passion for sports?" I've heard some parents scoff. "Heck, if I let them, my kids would play sports from sunup to sundown. They'd never stop."

It sure seems that way, doesn't it? Well, that kind of spirited fun is exactly what this book is about: making sure that your child hangs onto that same sort of enjoyment as he moves into organized sports at five or six, and continues to get the same sort of reward well into junior high school and beyond.

The passion for sports starts early and can last a lifetime.

A few years ago, a top college coach complained to me: "I've got an athlete with more physical talent and ability than anyone I've ever coached. But this kid plays the game like it's a job, or an obligation. He just doesn't seem to have any zest for what he's doing. . . . I don't understand how he can have so little fun playing a sport that he's so good at."

The problem? Like too many young athletes, somewhere along the way from playground to college arena, he lost his passion for the game.

To me, most kids lose this sense of passion early in their years of youth sports. And more often than not, we parents—especially well-meaning, concerned parents—are the reason the love affair with sports begins to dissipate.

Here's an example: Imagine that your eight-year-old is a talented soccer player. He scores lots of goals, is quick on the field, and seems to have a real feel for the game. He absolutely loves playing the game because he knows he's good at it.

Naturally, you take great pride in your son's abilities. It's clear to you and the other parents on the sidelines that he's a cut above the others—at least at his age. One day someone suggests that your child might benefit by playing on an elite, or travel, team. Now the competition is a little tougher on a travel team, but you figure that'll only make your son an even better player. Besides, he'll get a travel team

When kids love to play sports, sometimes it's hard to know how much is too much.

jacket and uniform, and he'll enjoy the prestige he deserves as a star player.

So you sign up your eight-year-old for the travel team.

But you and your kid soon discover that playing with a travel team isn't quite the same as playing for a neighborhood recreational team. For starters, your eight-year-old isn't playing with neighborhood pals anymore. Now he's playing with kids from all over. And instead of playing forward, as he did on his rec team, he's stuck on defense—a change he's not too keen on. Furthermore, because there are a number of extra players on the team, your kid now only plays about half the game, not the full game he's used to.

What happens to your kid when he goes from neighborhood star to travel team obscurity? Naturally, he becomes a bit shy and intimidated by the abrupt change in surroundings. Sensing this, concerned that your child is no longer the star but just one of the members of the team, you turn to the travel team coach for advice. The coach is sympathetic, and suggests the following: "Look, your boy is a fine player, but if he wants to be a star at this elite level, you should think about enrolling him in some extra soccer practices; they're held twice a week from 7:00 to 8:30 at night in one of the local gyms. After all, most of the other kids on the team do just that."

Your misgivings increase. You want only the best for your son, but as it stands the

Kids who play sports can find themselves under a lot of scrutiny—from parents, coaches, and fellow teammates.

travel team already has a demanding schedule of games—not to mention two or three practices per week. And the coach thinks you should tack on a couple more nights of practice per week?

Time for a little expert advice: Sit your eight-year-old kid down and ask him what he wants to do. "Well, I guess if the coach is suggesting that I do it, I ought to do it." Confident that your eight-year-old boy is making a well-informed, rational decision, you sign him up for the extra practice sessions.

For the next three months, your son sticks to a schedule that transforms him from a kid who plays soccer into a soccer player who happens to be a kid. But he still doesn't get to play any more than half the game—sometimes even a little less—and he's still playing a position he doesn't enjoy. What's more, now he has even less time for his old friends from school, what with games, practices, extra training, and all the shuttling back and forth.

Then, one day late in the season, your kid says: "Couldn't I just miss this one practice session? I just don't feel like going today. . . ."

And so it begins. Your kid's passion for soccer is starting to wither. Now this eight-year-old might very well bounce back the following year and recapture his love for the sport. But it's also possible that he ends up abandoning soccer entirely.

The sad irony is that you—his fictitious mom or dad—did everything you could in your son's best interest. You merely tried your very best to give the child every opportunity to explore his dream. Yet the result is that by age ten this child is on the brink of giving up on soccer entirely, saying that the sport is "boring" and that practices "are the worst."

SO WHAT WENT WRONG?

What turns an enjoyable and rewarding sport into drudgery? And what can you do to keep it from happening to your kid?

First off, you should know that it's a fairly common problem. In fact, according to a recent study, close to 80 percent of *all* kids stop playing organized youth sports by the time they're twelve. And it doesn't make any difference whether they're playing a team sport or an individual sport; the bottom line is that the vast majority simply stops playing.

Why do they stop? Usually for one of two rea-

Let Your Child Chase Her Dreams

Too often, parents who mean well will keep reminding a child that it's foolish to ever think that he or she will ever get a pro contract. So rather than "wasting time" in chasing that dream, they chide their children to "come back to reality" and put sports into perspective.

Don't be in such a rush to crush those dreams. Rather, remind them that while it's great to want to be a star quarterback in the NFL, they should also have lots of other dreams in life—just in case the dream of playing in the NFL doesn't work out.

Dot Richardson, the star shortstop of the U.S. Olympic softball team, also dreamed of becoming a doctor while chasing her dream of playing sports. She's now a practicing orthopedic surgeon. Tim Green, who was an All-American football player at Syracuse and NFL star for the Atlanta Falcons, also dreamed of becoming a writer when he was a kid. He had his first national best-seller published last year.

So don't feel so compelled as a grown-up to dash your child's passion for sports. Take a more positive approach. Explain to your child that there is no singular or direct pathway to success in life, but that the fun comes from chasing one's dreams to the fullest, no matter where those dreams might take you.

sons: either they're not enjoying sports enough or they're feeling too much pressure to succeed. And who's applying the pressure? Teammates, coaches, friends, siblings all play their part. More often than not, however, the pressure comes either directly or indirectly from Mom and Dad.

It's not difficult for a parent, even unconsciously, to transform a son's or daughter's fun and relaxing sports life into an endless series of daily chores and demands. It doesn't take much; after all, even a kid realizes that playing at a certain level results in pressure to perform well— pressure that often shoves fun off to one side.

Kids are keenly aware that, when they compete, not

After a game, kids crave attention and praise. Keep the constructive criticism for later.

only are Mom and Dad watching from the sidelines but so are a bunch of other parents as well as referees or umpires and a head coach, who's barking out instructions throughout the game. There may even be a scoreboard that constantly reminds everyone who's winning and who's losing.

What's more, a lot of young athletes jump into the family car after the game only to find themselves the featured guest on "Mom and Dad's Post-game Wrap-up Show." No sooner is the vehicle in gear than the first question comes: "Sally, how come the coach took you out of the game in the second quarter?" or "Michael, what happened when you booted that grounder in the third inning?"

If you've ever seen a pro athlete quail under such questioning, imagine how hard it is for a kid. Just when he should be cooling down from the rigors of the game, not only does he have to relive every moment of the contest but he's got to come up with a respectable answer for every miscue. And God forbid he shouldn't have a good reason for a misplay, because Mom or Dad might think it's the perfect time—"while the game is still fresh in the kid's mind"—to hand out a little constructive criticism.

THE KID'S POINT OF VIEW

Imagine how confused a kid can get under all this pressure. The last thing he heard before the game started was "have fun," not "play well and have fun if you can," not "make sure you don't embarrass yourself or me in front of the other parents, and by the way see if you can have some fun." It was just "have fun"—no other conditions or stipulations. Yet now that the game is over, nobody's talking about fun anymore. Instead, everyone's talking about who won and how well you played and what you did wrong and how you need a little more practice. Very few professional athletes would endure this kind of grilling; why would an eight- or nine-year-old want to hear it?

It's easy to see where this leads. After several appearances on "Mom and Dad's Post-game Wrap-up Show," a kid begins to develop conditioned responses to interrogation—just like the pros do. Either he simply ignores his parents' conversation on the way home (the way Eddie Murray has been ignoring the

Sports Parenting Skills Tip

Kids love wearing new sports uniforms and getting to use new sports equipment. Whenever your child gets on a team and is given a new team uniform, give her plenty of positive feedback about how cool she looks in her new duds. The same advice goes when kids get a new pair of soccer shoes, or baseball gloves, or a tennis racquet. Let them enjoy the moment!

press for years) or he gives automatic, monosyllabic answers just to get the interview over with. If he's really inventive he might borrow a few meaningless statements from real press conferences:

"I guess I left my game in the locker room."

"I need to give 110 percent next time."

"I didn't play my game; I played their game."

After a while, who could blame a kid for thinking that all this so-called "fun" isn't worth the criticism he receives? All he knows is that without the sport, there's no parental disapproval, no constructive criticism, no postgame analyses. Much better to hang out with friends, watch TV, or get a part-time job.

IS THIS "BURN OUT"?

Some parents call this alienation "burn-out." Their kid quits soccer or basketball or tennis because the demands of the game have worn him down—a regrettable but natural risk when a kid plays competitive sports. It's the same sort of burn-out felt by people in high-stress jobs: Wall Street types who abandon the rat race for life on a farm; Hollywood agents who decide they'll be happier pumping gas; cardiovascular surgeons who take up general practice in rural New England towns.

But do we really want our kids to run the risk of this sort of burn-out from playing *baseball*? Where does it say children should be subjected to the same sort of stress that drives us adults nuts?

$$\left(\text{\textit{"Competition and challenge are very different concepts."}} \right)$$

It's true that many kids do give up sports in favor of other interests—music, art, dating, or academics, to name a few. But when 80 percent of all kids give up sports before they become teenagers, something else is responsible: a loss of passion. Without that unrestricted love of athletics and sports, kids just give up.

You can help insure that your child continues to play the sport for all the right rea-

In the early years, sports is all about challenge.

sons. So when you tell your little one to go out on that playing field and "have fun," just make certain you mean it.

INSIDE TIPS

→ Before the age of nine, kids merely enjoy the fun of having a new uniform, being on the same team with school friends, and running around the field. Be lavish in your praise, ask what part of the game they enjoyed the most, and be sincerely supportive of their efforts.

→ Don't be so concerned about your child winning or losing in these early years. Competition is certainly part of the game, but there's plenty of time for the kids to learn about the realities of winning and losing as they get older.

What you *do* want your young athlete to experience is a sense of *challenge*. Recognize that competition and challenge are indeed very different concepts. You want your young children to be challenged by the skills of sports, so that

Learn from the Pros

When Grant Hill, the NBA superstar for the Detroit Pistons, was growing up in suburban Virginia, he suffered through what he called "postgame analyses." As Grant relates in his book, *Change the Game*, his dad—former NFL running back Calvin Hill—just couldn't wait until Grant got in the car to start a detailed analysis of the game Grant just played. These sessions, relates Grant, were sometimes painful and put an unnecessary strain on their relationship as father and son.

Parents be forewarned: Although Grant got through these postgame analyses and kept on playing, too many talented kids don't. They just give up playing the sport, rather than expose themselves to a grilling after each game. Don't assume that your child will be able to endure these analyses the way a Grant Hill did.

they can feel that they are making progress athletically and mastering these skills, whether it's hitting a tennis ball over a net or learning how to swim. As noted, there's plenty of time later to learn how to face and deal with competition. First, they have to experience the challenge of mastering sports.

→ If you feel your child's coach is taking things a bit too seriously, gently remind the coach that it's more important for the kids to have fun and enjoy themselves at young ages than to worry about which team wins the championship.

Look around at the end of each game. You'll see that even after a close game, the kids on each team will look depressed and upset . . . for about forty-five seconds, tops. Then they'll want to know if they can go for ice cream or whether they can go to a friend's house for a play date or whatever. For the kids, the game is history; now it's time to do something else. If there's any talk of a game, it's not the one just played, but the next one.

We parents would do well to follow our kids' example: once the game is over, win or lose, forget about it. Start looking forward to the next game. How's it going to look if your kid has to come over and cheer you up after his team loses? "Hey, it's not the end of the world, Dad. Cheer up. C'mon, I'll let you buy me a milk shake. . . ." If you find that you have a harder time dealing with wins and losses than your kid does, you need to step back, take a deep breath, and remember that when your kid says, "We won" or "We lost," he's talking about the team—not you.

→ To keep their passion alive for sports, try following these rules:

1. Children develop a passion for their sport when

Even when they've lost, kids usually bounce back readily after a game.

they're left alone to enjoy, develop, and master their skills in that sport—without the complicating factors of parental overview or approval.

2. Eliminate the postgame analysis; it can only damage your child's love for the sport.

3. Be wary of putting too much pressure on your child. Be careful of travel teams for kids any younger than ten.

There's nothing wrong with your eight-year-old taking pride in being a dominant player at an early age. There's plenty of time to step up against tougher competition as he or she gets older.

DID YOU KNOW?

In Canada, where kids lace up ice skates as soon as they can walk, enthusiasm for active participation in hockey drops off precipitously by the time kids reach adolescence. According to a poll undertaken by the Canadian Amateur Hockey Asociation, by the time Canadian kids turn fifteen, only about one out of every ten is still playing organized youth hockey. The others have given up the sport.

PLAYING THE FIELD: LETTING YOUR CHILD EXPERIMENT WITH SPORTS

Consider the following:

→ Hakeem Olajuwon, seven-foot-tall center and perennial NBA All-Star, former MVP of his league, didn't start playing basketball until he was almost seventeen years old. Until then, Hakeem's favorite sport was soccer, where he was a star goalkeeper.

→ National League All-Star outfielder Larry Walker didn't start playing baseball seriously until he was sixteen years old—and he took it up only after he gave up on his first sports dream: playing in the National Hockey League.

→ Grant Hill, the NBA All-Star, was an outstanding soccer forward in elementary and junior high school. Only when he reached high school (at the age of fifteen) did he decide to concentrate solely on hoops.

→ Atlanta Braves pitcher Tom Glavine, winner of the 1991 Cy Young Award, was drafted straight out of his Massachusetts high school—by the Los Angeles Kings of the National Hockey League.

→ Kenny Lofton, the outstanding major league center fielder, didn't really start playing serious baseball until his college career was almost over; he'd been specializing in basketball!

→ And let's not forget all the great two-sport stars of today, like Deion Sanders and Jackie Joyner-Kersee. Remember Bo Jackson's double career in football and baseball? Did you know that Danny Ainge, the former NBA star and now coach, used to play in the majors for the Toronto Blue Jays? Or that pitcher Orel Hershiser, a scratch golfer, has seriously thought about playing professional golf once his baseball career is over?

These top athletes, and many others like them, enjoyed a variety of sports well into adolescence before concentrating on making a living playing just one (or two, in the cases of Deion Sanders and Bo Jackson). There's no reason your own kid can't enjoy the same variety. If he's going to end up a pro some day, it's not going to hold

34

Children enjoy the challenge of playing many different kinds of sports.

him back. And if he's destined to be a weekend enthusiast, playing different sports is just plain fun.

You don't have to narrow your child's attention down to one sport. It's true that in certain sports—gymnastics, figure skating, swimming—the earlier a kid begins to concentrate on one discipline, the better the chances of excelling in that sport. But to me, that always begs the question: How do you know which sport is going to be the best for your five-year-old child?

Unless you're clairvoyant, that's a tough question to answer. There's just no way you can determine which sport will best fit your kid's needs and talents—or, more importantly, your kid's passion. The point isn't to identify the sport your kid can play professionally or the game he shows the best natural aptitude for. Rather, it's the sport he is passionate about. (Fun, remember?)

To complicate matters even more, most athletically inclined children like to play different kinds of sports. Ask any eight- or ten-year-old what her favorite sport is to play. Chances are she'll just shrug her shoulders and say: "All

It is natural for parents to try to pass on their love of a particular sport to their children. But children discover their own favorite sports, too.

36

of them!" And for most kids, that's the truth.

So let your kid try as many different sports as he wants—soccer, roller-blading, gymnastics, softball, badminton—whatever captures his fancy.

$$\left(\quad \textit{"If your child wants to go out for curling, so be it."} \quad \right)$$

If she decides to take up a sport you don't know much about, learn about it together. Rather than trying to push your child into a sport that you played (and want to relive through your kid) or are more familiar with, let her find her own pathway to fun. It's her life, after all. If she wants to get into curling, so be it. The least you can do, as a supportive parent, is learn the sport with her. (If she ever gives up on the game, you can always use a few more brooms around the house.)

PERSONAL EXAMPLE NO. 1

Six years ago, when he was about seven years old, my son John fell in love with ice hockey. It was a bit of shock to me; after all, I couldn't even ice-skate. But it was my son's decision to make, not mine; and when I realized his love of the sport was for real, I bought myself a pair of ice skates. At the advanced age of forty-two, I learned how to skate: my son taught me!

Now, I still don't skate very well, but that isn't the point. Because I took it upon myself to learn how to skate, I get to share in the joy my son feels whenever he skates. Better yet, once in a while he even coaches me when I take to the ice—and helps me up when I hit it.

WELCOME TO TODAY!

One of the nicer aspects about life in the 1990s is that both boys and girls have a much wider array of sports to play. Television has exposed a generation of kids to sports like roller-blading, snow-boarding, mountain biking, skate-boarding, and the dozens of more competitive sports we see in the Olympics. (You can make up your own mind whether bungee-jumping is a sport or an accident waiting to happen.)

Should a Child Specialize in Just One Sport?

David Hemery, 1968 Olympic gold medalist in the 400-meter hurdles, interviewed sixty-three of the greatest athletes for his book, *In Pursuit of Sporting Excellence*. Of those athletes, Hemery found that only five specialized in just one sport before the age of twelve. The average age at which these athletes began focusing on just one sport was sixteen.

This is all good news, because kids instinctively *like* to try different kinds of competitive activities. They like the challenge of trying to ride a snow board, race on a bicycle, or see just how fast they are in the water. And the more sports a kid tries, the greater her chance of finding a particular sport or two that she really loves.

Does this mean that you have an annual obligation to sign your kid up for every sporting activity offered by the local recreation department or YMCA? No, of course not. But what you can—and should—do is to simply sit down with your six- or eight- or ten-year-old and ask her what sports she'd like to play during the upcoming semester.

Usually your child will prefer to participate in sporting events with friends. And why not? Just be careful not to lock your child into one sport *all the time*. Such a commitment can often lead a child to boredom with that sport ("Do I have to go to soccer practice again this week?"), and in some cases, can even lead to burn-out.

If you do encounter this kind of resistance, then the time has probably come for a little chat with your child about whether he's really having fun with the sport. Kids often surprise us with how honest and candid their responses can be.

CASE STUDY NO. 1: DON'T LOCK ONTO ONE SPORT TOO EARLY

I remember talking to the father of a ten-year-old who boasted that his son was playing on not just one but three hockey teams at the same time. When I wondered how his son could possibly find the time for that much hockey,

There are many new sports, like indoor rock climbing, that have become popular with kids across the United States.

No matter how talented he is, be careful of locking your child into one sport too early.

  Sports Parenting Skills Tip

Injuries are part of the game. Whether it's a skinned knee or a bump on the head, kids do occasionally get hurt playing sports. The way in which you react to these injuries can have a major impact on how kids themselves react to them. So be attentive, be sympathetic, and be careful. But avoid going to extremes: don't treat minor injuries as catastrophic and by all means, don't ignore them.

the father explained that the boy played hockey every day after school (except Mondays). That's some grind for anyone, let alone a fifth-grader!

(*"Many athletic skills are transferable from one sport to another."*)

Now, this boy's parents weren't crazy or socially inadequate people. To the contrary, they were well-educated professionals, deeply concerned with their son's well-being. They had evidently decided that their son was going to be a hockey player. And in their minds, the best way to give him a "jump up" on other hockey playing kids was to keep him playing all the time—if possible, year round.

I asked Dad how he had determined at such an early age that his son's best sport was ice hockey. His response? "Because that's the sport he plays."

I felt the father had missed the point of my question, and repeated: How had Dad determined that hockey was his son's best sport?

"His best sport is ice hockey," came the reply, "because that's HIS sport."

Now, that sort of circular reasoning usually spells disaster. The chances were that whatever lay at the heart of this incredible commitment, it wasn't the boy's best interests. At ten, the kid was less a hockey enthusiast than a hockey machine. A few months ago I bumped into that same father and asked how his son (who's now fourteen) was progressing with his ice hockey career.

"Well, actually, he's not playing hockey this year," admitted the father. "He discovered girls last year, and just doesn't seem to have the same enthusiasm for hockey as he used to."

I quickly changed the subject.

CASE STUDY NO. 2: "THIS SPORT I PLAY FOR FUN . . ."

I was once asked to work with a gifted eight-year-old tennis player who, according to his parents, needed a little performance enhancement. Watching the child play, I could see that he was, indeed, very good.

Although I advised the parents that it was a little early to start thinking about

spending their life savings on specialized tennis lessons, coaches, equipment, and training aids, I could see that they were already fantasizing about their son playing at Forest Hills.

My misgivings grew when I spoke with the boy privately. He confided that "I play other sports like soccer and baseball just for fun. But tennis I play for real."

When I asked him to explain the difference, he replied: "Some sports I do because there's no pressure on me to have to win or do well, like baseball or soccer. But in tennis—well, I'm supposed to win."

When I repeated some of these thoughts to Mom and Dad, they were astonished: "I wonder where he got that idea?" they said. "After all, he knows that we have him concentrate on tennis only because he's so good at it. . . . We really don't put any pressure on him."

The bottom line? In both cases, the parents were not crazy, win-at-all-costs ogres but caring people who merely wanted the best for their children. Even so, they lost track of the overriding goal of their children's sports life: to have fun.

It happens everywhere. It may even be happening to your kid. Ask yourself: *When I talk with my child about sports, do I unintentionally put the pressure on to achieve? Does my child play only in order to please me and my spouse? Is my only agenda the amount of enjoyment my kid gets out of sports?*

SO AT WHAT AGE SHOULD A CHILD SPECIALIZE?

OK, so when should you worry about having your kid concentrate on just one sport?

You shouldn't worry at all. Most kids will answer that question for themselves, without any help from you. By the time they hit junior high, homework, part-time jobs, and other extracurricular activities start to crowd out all but one or two sports anyway—and most kids naturally gravitate to the sports they're good at, those they enjoy, or a combination of both. (For a parent, it's really a no-brainer.)

To find out more about kids and sports, go to www.trainingcamp.com

Swimming may be the one truly mandatory sport. Not only is it socially essential, but it also saves lives.

DID YOU KNOW?

According to a recent report from the Consumer Products Safety Commission, almost 75 percent of all baseball injuries occurred to children ages ten to fourteen. The highest number of baseball-related injuries occur to eleven- and twelve-year-olds.

With baseball-playing kids ages five to seven, the most common injury was a facial one, caused by a pitched ball, a batted ball, or trying to catch a thrown ball.

Is My Child the Next Tiger Woods or Martina Hingis?

In a few selected sports, because the athlete peaks as early as the middle or late teens, it's essential that the child start specializing early in life in order to make the most of her potential.

This topic is more fully examined in chapter nine about individual sports, but to give you a brief preview, you have to answer three basic questions about your child:

1. Is your child really that good? Ask the local coaches and experts. Don't let your emotions lead you.

2. Check with your physician. Most experts in gymnastics, skating, and tennis ask whether the youthful star is going to put on weight during adolescence, which, of course, can have a major impact on the child's career.

3. Do you fully understand the cost—both financial and emotional—that your family and your child is going to go through? For example, according to several news stories regarding the graceful teenaged Tara Lipinski, the top American figure skater, her parents spent more than $50,000 a year on Tara's skating lessons and putting her on the tour. That meant taking Tara out of her local school and, in order to pay the bills, getting a second mortgage on the house. Tara's mother travels with her all over while her dad works and stays at home in Houston, Texas.

This is not an extreme case. Tara's case tends to be typical for those families who want to allow their child to try and reach for the gold ring in sports. Sadly, for every Tara Lipinski or Tiger Woods, there are dozens more whose dreams never come true.

It's not surprising that most kids are drawn to activities that raise their sense of self-esteem and pleasure. It explains why a big-for-his-age, heavyset kid might be more interested in playing football than in trying to keep up with his quicker, faster peers on a soccer field. Or why the tall, gangly thirteen-year-old girl decides to stay with basketball rather than compete on the gymnastics squad. Or why the small, wiry lad decides to go out for wrestling. Or the fast runner goes out for track.

Most of the time, all you have to do is stay out of the way. If your kid comes to you for advice, feel free to point out the pros and cons of various sports. But remember that it's up to your kid—he's usually the best judge of his best sport.

ARE ATHLETIC SKILLS TRANSFERABLE?

Getting your kid to specialize becomes even less of an issue if you realize that most athletic skills are transferable from one sport to another. Speed is speed, whether it's used to start a fast break on a basketball court or to steal second base on a baseball diamond. The wrist strength built by practicing slap shots comes in quite handy in swinging a baseball bat. The same quick footwork needed to maneuver a soccer ball upfield is a real help on a tennis court.

"But the sooner my kid learns how to shoot a basketball properly or learns how to serve a tennis ball," say many moms and dads, "the better off he'll be. That's the key to later success in the sport."

No argument there. Of course a child benefits from practicing particular sports skills. That's the

Athletic skills involving speed and strength are readily transferable from one sport to another.

essence of coaching. But there's no reason why kids can't be taught how to do things properly in *all* the various sports they play.

INSIDE TIPS

→ *Learn the rules with your kids.* If you're unfamiliar with the rules of the sport your children are playing, head over to the local library for a primer on the sport. Lots of kids today play soccer, a sport which, for many American parents, is still difficult to understand (especially the offsides rule). Why not check out a library book on soccer rules and read it with your child before bed time? You'll end up educating yourself as well as your kid.

→ *Let them come to you.* When your children come to you for guidance about a certain sport, that's the time to focus on how much they enjoy it, and whether they truly want to continue it. As they reach the age of eleven or older, they'll see for themselves the essence of competitive sports. It's during these ages that you can help with the decision to continue in a particular sport or to try some other ones.

04

PRAISE: THE BEST MOTIVATOR

The most powerful motivator for kids in sports isn't success, popularity, or status—it's praise.

Praise can let a kid know he's on the right track, raise the spirits of a struggling player, and take the sting out of losing.

But giving praise isn't as easy as you might think; you can't just hand out raves indiscriminately. Kids learn how to spot insincerity pretty quickly. It's not enough to be generous with praise; you have to mean what you say. And the tone of your voice says as much as your words, so keep an ear out for the way you sound. It's all too easy for your words to say, "Nice play, kid," while your tone says, "What good did it do us? We lost!"

There's a right and a wrong way to hand out praise. In fact, you'd be surprised how many coaches don't even know that. Here's an example: A six-year-old is having a difficult time learning how to catch a thrown ball.

Coach A's approach: "Come on, Julie, we'll wait for you. You're bound to get the knack of it . . . eventually."

Coach B's approach: "You're almost there, Julie. Just stay with it—you're definitely getting the hang of this tricky business."

The difference is obvious: although Coach A believes he's encouraging Julie, the message he's really sending is: "Your inability to catch is holding up the whole team, but we'll stand here and watch you screw up as long as it takes." What he considers praise actually undermines Julie's confidence. It wouldn't be surprising if she eventually quit rather than be a burden to her teammates.

Now Coach B also believes that he's encouraging Julie—and he's right. Rather than emphasize her weakness, he praises her progress, voices confidence in her eventual success, and mentions that what she's doing is no easy task. How could she fail to take heart?

Good coaches know how to communicate real and sincere praise to young athletes.

Parents who gain their children's confidence by handing out just the right combination of praise and constructive criticism can make a positive difference in their kids' attitude towards sports.

GIVING A BITE OF A "PRAISE" SANDWICH

Praise is an important tool for helping your kid improve his play. Here's an approach that works:

Suppose you've identified some facet of your child's game that needs improvement—and that you've got the know-how to help him straighten out the problem. How can you bring up the subject without raining on your kid's parade?

First, remember not to pounce on him right after the latest game. Wait until you've both put the game behind you, and then start off with a slice of praise: "Hey Jamie, you really played a great game today. You've gotten to be a brilliant ball handler". That's the first slice of praise. If it is sincere, you now have your child's attention.

Now comes the meat of the sandwich: "And you know, Jamie, once you learn how to look up while you dribble the ball, you'll be unstoppable." (See how your constructive criticism still manages to convey confidence in your kid's ability to improve?)

And what sandwich would be complete without another slice of praise: "Jamie, if you continue to work hard and improve your game, why, you'll be some kind of soccer player."

It's the perfect recipe: take two-thirds praise, one-third well-couched constructive criticism, and what do you get? A kid who not only feels great about her abilities, but is inspired to work on improving them. Now that's nutrition!

SARCASM: THE OTHER (EVIL) END OF THE SPECTRUM

As long as we're on the subject of praise, I feel it's important to warn you about something that can kill a kid's enthusiasm as easily as praise builds it up: sarcasm.

Kids—especially those between the ages of four and nine or ten—simply don't understand sarcasm. They're just not old enough to understand that your cynical wise-crack about their skill, effort, or ability is supposed to be funny. Instead, while you get a great big laugh out of your grown-up joke, they take what you're saying at face value—and it hurts.

Think I'm kidding? Imagine how your eight-year-old would respond to a comment like: "Hey, Eric, any chance at all of you passing the ball to one of your teammates today?" How about: "Now, Sally, you're a lot bigger than most of the girls on the other team. So when you knock them down today, don't knock them down too hard."

You get the drift. Even if you think you're the funniest coach this side of Rodney Dangerfield, remember who's listening to you—and save those sarcastic comments for your memoirs.

"Wash Out" Syndrome

Too many young athletes stop playing youth sports either because they fail to make the team or because they're made to feel that they aren't good enough to succeed. A substantial body of research suggests the kids who do stop playing sports do so not because the sport isn't enjoyable but because there's such an emphasis on winning.

PRAISE THE EFFORT, NOT THE OUTCOME

We adults know that young athletes come in all sizes and shapes and with various levels of ability—and that generally a team will have a few outstanding players, a few weak players, and a whole bunch of average Joes.

But although you and I see the big picture that way, the kids on any given team have a rather different perspective. You'd be hard pressed to find a kid who didn't think he was one of the better players on his team. If you don't believe me, take an informal poll of the players on your team. You'll be amazed at how many top players you'll find!

How do you praise a kid who thinks he's one of the best players around, but whose efforts aren't paying off? How do you avoid bursting his bubble?

By praising the effort, not the outcome, such as:

➜ "Julie, I just want you to know that I'm totally impressed with the effort you're putting forth on this team."

➜ "Jack, there's no question that you've established yourself as one of the hardest workers in practice. "

➜ "Chris, with the kind of determination you've showed, why, you've made tremendous progress this season."

Praising the effort in this way makes a kid feel good about her efforts and hard work, and lets her know that her coach or parent sees how hard she's been working. And since it focuses on effort, not results, you'll never end up trying to praise your kid for running the wrong way with the ball.

BE CAREFUL OF THE MESSAGE

Tying praise to effort, not results, also helps coaches and parents avoid placing too much emphasis on winning. Too many games end with speeches like these:

➜ "I'm really disappointed in you kids today. All you had to do was pay a little more attention to the game plan, and you could have won."

➜ "I just wish you guys had taken this game a little more seriously today—because iif you had, you could have easily won."

To find out more about kids and sports, go to www.trainingcamp.com

Such comments confuse six- and seven-year-old kids, who—after spending an hour running around with friends and having fun—discover that they've done something wrong. They've lost. It doesn't take long for kids to realize that, for their parents, winning, not fun, is the priority. So remember that the emphasis should be on active participation (regardless of ability) and fun. Kids can learn about coping with winning and losing as they get older, but when they're younger than ten, it's just not the time to make winning a priority.

COMMUNICATION IS THE KEY

For coaches (and parents who coach), a major part of giving praise is building a rapport with your kids. To that end, take a tip from the world of business management: coach by walking around. For years, "Management by Walking Around" has been an invaluable method of building trust, respect, and rapport between managers and employees. That same principle is used by many top

Parents should praise their child's effort, not just how well he does.

 Sports Parenting Skills Tip

Teaching your child how to ride a bicycle is one of the great joys of parenthood. Yet the first few times on a bike can be a little unsettling for any child. Training wheels are a must until your kid tells you he wants to try his luck on a two-wheeler. And when that day arrives (usually around the age of five or six), find a clear, level road or track, sit him on the bike, and then walk (or run) right next to him to keep him from falling.

Yes, it might take a few lessons and some assists from you, but eventually he'll get the hang of it. By the way, make it part of the lesson that your son or daughter never get on a bike without putting on a safety helmet first.

→ When John Franco, top relief ace for the New York Mets, was a freshman in high school, he was five-foot-four and weighed less than a hundred pounds. Although Franco was a terrific pitcher, his high school coach took one look at him and said: "Come back when you've grown up." Franco was crushed by the callous remark, but never gave up on himself. He's been a big league star for well over a decade, and yes—he now stands five-eleven and weighs 180 pounds.

→ When former NFL star running back Roger Craig was first playing tackle football in Davenport, Iowa, at age eight, he was so afraid of getting hurt that he refused to tackle or block anybody.

→ Warren Moon, the great NFL quarterback, remembers distinctly the day when the coach of his youth league football team advised him: "You stink!" Recalls Moon: "The coach yelled it so loud that everyone heard it. My whole team and everyone in the stands heard the coach say it. It hurt me badly."

Kids always respond to individual attention and encouragement.

professional and college coaches in order to reach their athletes.

As a coach, all you have to do is wander around during practice and make certain you spend as little as a minute or two with each child on the team, addressing each one by name, handing out little pats on the back, and praising the effort they're making. Kids are thrilled when coaches devote even as little as a minute of their time on some personal attention. The personal interest you show in them and their progress pays off as the season progresses; they'll listen more carefully to your advice and respond more quickly to instruction. Coaching by walking around is a solid approach to reaching athletes of all ages.

INSIDE TIPS

→ *Remember this about praise:*
Praise is simple, easy to give, and easily replenishable. And above everything else, that's what a child wants to hear from you. After all, it's what we grown-ups want to hear, too!

→ *Does it work?* Yes, praise *does* work. Most kids do believe in themselves; they just need their coach (or Mom or Dad) to believe in them also.
A true story: A year or so ago, I was coaching a

Praise your beginning athlete—and see how her self-confidence soars!

bunch of ten-year-old baseball players, one of whom played the game quite reluctantly. He didn't even want to go to practice, but he claimed his parents forced him. Although he was larger than the other kids, his whole persona indicated that he had been told over the years that he just wasn't very good at the game. Eventually, it became a self-fulfilling perception: he wouldn't hustle, didn't try to hit the ball very aggressively, didn't try to catch the ball, and so on.

I made him my special project for the year. I started to praise him early in the season, working with him and his batting stroke and his running, telling him how much potential power he had because he was a big kid, and so on. At first he didn't buy it, but once he realized that I wasn't going to give up on him, he began to develop some confidence. Even better, he realized that his teammates weren't poking fun at him; they figured that if I thought he could play, well, maybe he actually could.

By the middle of the season, the boy began to blossom. He went to bat with a newfound sense of confidence, and although he wasn't the best hitter on the team, he certainly got his share of hits. His teammates respected him, and, of course, he respected himself. He had done something for himself: he had accomplished a goal that he thought he never could.

By the end of the baseball season, this kid not only found that he enjoyed baseball but he was now the first kid at practice and the last one to leave. He had truly found a new passion in life, all because someone had taken a little time to encourage him.

Does this mean I'm a genius at working with kids? No. In fact, the beauty of this whole experience is that it's so easily duplicated in any town around the country—and with any kid. If you don't believe me, just try it yourself. Try praise and encouragement. You'll be amazed with the results.

05

"I JUST CAN'T DO IT": WHAT TO DO WHEN YOUR KID GETS FRUSTRATED

Everyone who plays sports has to deal with frustration.

This is true whether you're an accomplished superstar like Michael Jordan or just Michelle, a fifth grader on a girls' Saturday morning recreational team. Jordan feels the sting of frustration when he misses a key jump shot in a playoff game (incredible as that may seem) or if he makes an errant pass to a teammate. Michelle feels it when she misses an easy layup or if she doesn't get enough playing time in a game against her peers.

In other words, the sting of frustration is universal in sports—and it makes little difference whether you're Michael Jordan or little Michelle.

For a parent, sometimes the pain of frustration can be even more intense. After all, as a mom or dad, you want so badly for your kids to do their best, to be rewarded for their effort. You vicariously feel their pain when they miss that layup, have to sit on the bench, or don't make a particular play as well as some of the others. But all you can do is stand on the sidelines and suffer, try to hold back your own emotions, and hope that your child will somehow be able to turn frustration into personal motivation.

Unfortunately, some of us just can't control our own frustration. We've all seen and heard these parents. (Perhaps you're one of them yourself.) You can find them at every youth league game, pacing up and down, finally giving voice to their inner pain, attempting to "cheer" their kid to better performance with some version of the following:

➜ "C'mon, Johnny, you gotta play harder than that!"

➜ "Gee-zus kee-rist, Samantha, stop taking those terrible shots!"

➜ "Hey, Coach, when are you going to play *all* the kids on the team—and not just your favorites? "

Inspiring, isn't it? You get the idea. In a sense, I feel for these parents, because their deep frustration is so obvious—so much so that they think the only way to handle

Frustration is inevitable in sports.

it properly is by venting it in public. But it's their kids I really feel for.

When your child is frustrated, first help him identify the source of his frustration.

When it comes to youth sports, frustration comes in two flavors: the child's, and the parent's.

The child's frustration: As I said earlier, every kid who plays sports gets frustrated at some point. Frustration is built into sports. After all, if everything in sports were easy, then there wouldn't be any challenge to it, and without any challenge, where's the sense of accomplishment or mastery that goes with it? Experiencing frustration is a natural part of participating. Sure, some kids pick up the sport a little quicker than others, but even these more "athletically gifted" kids get frustrated, albeit at a slighter higher level of performance.

As a parent, you can help your kid with a three-step approach to any frustrating problem:

1. Isolate the frustrating activity.
2. Break down that activity into its basic parts.
3. Work with your child to overcome frustration, with equal parts of patience and praise.

That's a little general, so let's take a specific example. Suppose your eight-year-old daughter is having trouble learning to use both feet to maneuver a soccer ball. As a result, she always dribbles and shoots with her right foot. She's even mentioned that a few of her teammates already know how to dribble and shoot with either foot. What's worse, her coach has pointed out this problem to her.

Then, one day in a game, she misses what should have been an easy left-footed goal because she uses her right foot instead. Her frustration is both obvious and heart-wrenching; she's depressed and embarrassed at having let down her team.

What can you do? The next day (never right after the game!) ask your daughter if she'd like to go outside and kick a soccer ball with you. Keep it that simple, too. The last thing she wants to hear is your master plan for conquering her little footwork problem. And if she doesn't want to go outside and play, just go outside and start playing by yourself—or, better yet, with some of the other neighborhood kids. The exercise is good for you, and within a few minutes your kid might miraculously show up to join in. (Kids can't stand being left out of the fun.)

In any event, once the two of you are playing soccer, gently ask her about her frustration from the day before. She'll probably talk about the lack of skill at dribbling with both feet.

The first step is over: the two of you have identified and isolated the frustration.

You accomplish step two, breaking down that activity into manageable parts, by setting up some very simple drills for you to do together. To learn how to dribble with the left foot, for example, suggest a game of one-on-one soccer with your daughter in which she can only dribble and shoot with her left foot.

Step three is nothing more than remembering to keep your praise high and your critical comments to a real low. Encourage her. Tell her how much progress she's making. Hopefully, she'll be so thrilled with her increasing dribbling ability that she'll want to come back the next day and do it again. Once you've reached that level of self-motivation, you know that your child is on her way to improving herself as an athlete—and enhancing her sense of self-esteem.

 ### *Sports Parenting Skills Tip*

Baseball is one of the most difficult sports for young people to play. Why? For starters, they have to have a number of skills: being able to catch a ball, hit it, field it, run the bases, and so on. Naturally kids can become easily frustrated. To help overcome their fear of the ball, use a Flexiball or Softeeball when they're starting out. Play catch with young children by gently tossing them the ball only a few feet apart. Make certain they catch the ball with both hands. Only gradually try and step back a little further, but don't lengthen the space between you and your child until he or she can actually catch the ball consistently.

There may be times in sports when your child just isn't enjoying herself.

The parent's frustration: Parents watching from the sidelines or the stands go through their own brand of frustration.

Most parents are pretty good at keeping things in perspective—acting the role of grown-ups at a kids' game. But there are those times when a parent just can't deal with the frustration anymore, and starts yelling at his child, the coach, the officials, the opposing players, the parents of the opposing players, his spouse, and anyone else within earshot.

If you're ever tempted to do this, try to remember that there's a better way to get your point across than throwing a fit. Nobody—coaches, refs, and especially kids—ever responds in a positive way to a parent's tantrum. What's more, it won't be long before your community pins a "First-class Loudmouth and Ill-Mannered Jerk" label on you—and such a label is pretty hard to live down. And even if you're willing to accept such a label in order to get your kid the sports justice he deserves, consider what really happens when you give in to your frustrations:

➜ The coach concludes that you're just another hot-headed parent who only cares about his or her child and nobody else—certainly not the sport.

➜ The official immediately becomes defensive about his or her calls in the game, and dismisses you as a meddling dolt.

➜ Your child (who has to watch you lose your cool) is blatantly embarrassed in front of his friends and friends' parents, and ends up saying things like: "My parents? Are you kidding? I've never seen them before in my life!"

➜ Finally, when your tantrum is over, you have that lovely realization that you've made a complete jackass out of yourself. Yes, every other parent probably felt the same way as you did, but you're the only one who couldn't control himself. You can only take solace in the fact that you've just provided many of them with a valuable lesson about how not to act at their kids' games—to say nothing of the endless neighborhood scuttlebutt you'll inspire.

To find out more about kids and sports, go to www.trainingcamp.com

You can set up simple drills to help your child improve his skills and overcome his frustration.

Naturally, you'd like your child to learn such values as "commitment" and "dedication" when she plays youth sports. Parents don't want their kid to quit when the going gets tough. But it's also important to apply common sense.

While you should always sit down with your child and explain what it means to join a team ("You have to follow the team rules, like going to practice and being on time . . ."), you should also realize that there will be times when your kid just isn't enjoying himself.

(*"The sting of frustration is universal."*)

Perhaps he's not ready yet for this level of competition. Perhaps none of his friends are on the team. Perhaps he just doesn't enjoy the game that much. Whatever the pressing reason, before you allow your child to quit the team, first you have to find out why he wants to stop playing.

Why this step? Many times a child sees quitting as the only way out of a frustrating situation. But you can avoid that drastic and often unnecessary decision by first discussing why she wants to quit. If she wants out only because of a temporary frustration, you can probably help her through it without giving up on the game. And if discussing the situation in depth reveals that your kid simply hates the sport, leaving the team isn't a bad idea. Just remember to give the coach a call and explain why the child is opting to leave. That's only fair. Then help your kid find some other sport where the frustrations are fewer and the fun is greater.

Kids often cry when they lose, or when they're frustrated or unhappy. It's perfectly natural.

INSIDE TIPS

→ *Turning lemons into lemonade:* Remind your child that there are literally thousands of top athletes who had to deal with frustration when they were kids. Every schoolchild knows that Michael Jordan was cut from his high school basketball team as a sophomore. Yet instead of giving up, Jordan used the sting of frustration as motivation to improve.

In fact, there are very few top athletes who weren't, at some point in their young athletic career, frustrated by some event or series of events. When Scottie Pippen was a high school senior, he thought he was such a good basketball player that he'd get lots of scholarship offers. Yet the only offer he received was from a small college —to be the equipment manager on the basketball team.

The truth here is a simple one: as a parent, it's up to you to encourage and work with your child to deal with anger and transform it into a positive motivation. There are lots of character-building aspects of sport, such as team play, discipline, and sportsmanship, but learning how to cope with— and master—frustration is definitely one of those skills that can be applied to all aspects of life. It's that important.

→ *Are kids allowed to cry?* Of course! There's nothing wrong with a kid who cries when frustrated or unhappy, especially kids under ten. It would be odd if a kid didn't cry under stressful circumstances. Eventually, kids learn to hold back their tears—not from their parents, but from their peers.

The bottom line? There's no need for you, as a parent, to chastise or embarrass a child who breaks into tears during a sporting event. Kids cry. It's no big deal.

→ *"I'm Worried About Your Child Getting Hurt":* What should you do when a coach balks at playing your kid because he's afraid your child might get hurt? "I can't put your son at first base. He just doesn't catch too well, and I'm afraid he's going to get hit in the face with a ball." Or, "Your son's a good skater, Mr. Smith, but he's just too small to play on this team. Sooner or later one of the bigger kids is going to check him into the boards, and he's going to get hurt."

Such coaches are just looking out for the best interests of the child. After all, if a kid goes out and gets hurt in one of the above situations, it's too easy for a parent to say: "Well, the coach must be a real dope. Anybody could see that the child wasn't ready to play first base. Anybody know a good lawyer?"

If you think your child isn't getting a chance to play because the coach fears for his safety, have a chat with the coach. Try to come to a consensus about your child's ability and the risk involved. If you feel strongly that your child can play first base, and should be given a chance there, then at least the coach knows that he can place your child there with your full blessing and responsibility.

DID YOU KNOW?

It's clear from the Consumer Products Safety Commission's research that using a softer, spongy safety baseball is much less dangerous with kids age five to ten. Unfortunately, very few youth baseball leagues use these safety balls: while soft baseballs represented 10 percent of the youth baseball market, they were involved in only 3 percent of all reported injuries.

Do the Pros Let Their Kids Play?

Larry Csonka made a stellar name for himself as a bruising, no-nonsense football fullback at Syracuse University and later with the NFL's Miami Dolphins. Nobody was tougher on a football field than Csonka.

But football fans might be surprised to discover that Csonka wouldn't allow his own two boys to play youth league football. Why not? Explains Csonka: "The coaches didn't know much about what they were doing. They just yelled a lot. They acted like they imagined Lombardi and Shula would act. Why, they had those eight-year-olds running gassers [long wind sprints], for crying out loud."

Continues the former NFL great: "The whole country loves football, and so do I. But parents don't stop to consider all the things that can go wrong for a young fellow pushed into that kind of pressure. For one thing, he can come home with a handful of teeth. Worse, he can come home soured on athletics for life."

06

WINNERS AND LOSERS:
HOW TO PREPARE YOUR KID FOR COMPETITION

Whether we like it or not, competition is a fact of life—and sooner or later, your kid is going to discover how much fun it is to win and just how rotten it is to lose. Youth sports provides you with a tremendous opportunity to introduce your child to competition in a kind, thoughtful manner and to show him how to prepare for and handle either eventuality.

Competition tends to make us protective of our children. We all know the flip side of "Who won?" and don't want our kid to feel like a loser. It's pretty tough to send your kid off to a game, only to see him come home with tears running down his cheeks. But hard as it is, it's simply part of growing up.

The real question isn't how you can *shield* your children from the emotional risks of competition, but how best to *prepare* them for it. Let's start with one simple rule: *the younger the kids, the less emphasis on competition.*

Kids from four to six years old have such a limited understanding of their sport that terms like "winning" and "losing" have very little meaning to them. Watch a bunch of five-year-olds play basketball sometime, and notice how everybody jumps up and down whenever a basket is scored—no matter who makes the basket. Who's winning? Who cares? It's enough that somebody managed to put the ball through the hoop.

The most important thing to these kids isn't the final score, but the simple shared joy of playing. Why ruin it with talk of winners and losers? They'll find out soon enough. Until then, forget league standings and playoff games. You can even forget keeping score of the games. If your kids don't care, why should you? (If you happen to spot a parent on the sidelines who seems to care an awful lot about who wins, feel free to butt in with: "They're just little kids. Who cares which team wins?")

By the time kids are seven or eight, they'll know how to keep score in a game. What they won't know is how to deal with what the score means; that is, how to cope with winning and losing.

Kids, like this boy who has just scored a goal, know just how much fun it is to win.

Kids soon learn that for every winner, there's also a loser.

In my experience, parents have a harder time dealing with losing than their kids do. Even a child who dissolves in tears after a losing effort bounces back after a few hugs and words of reassurance. Kids are amazingly resilient. Just a few minutes after that tearful, devastating loss, that same child is now skipping off to a playdate with a friend from the other team or looking forward to a birthday party later that day.

As kids grow older and their sporting events become more competitive, they begin to understand that for every winner, there's also going to be a loser—which is fine, as long as it's the other team that loses. Unfortunately, one day they're bound to look up at the scoreboard at the end of the game and realize that today they're the losers. That's where sportsmanship comes in.

The concept of sportsmanship rests upon the premise that victory is never a given, and that both sides should respect the sincere effort of their opponents. Since today's victors may be next week's losers—a risk that comes with any sporting event—the true essence of sport lies not in the final tally, but in the way the game itself is played. The practice of sportsmanship is an expression of civility; an acknowledgment that win or lose, each opponent recognizes the value, challenge, and fun of the competition that the other has provided for the day.

It stands to reason that since sportsmanship is so good for us, it's not something we're naturally good at. It's much easier to sulk, sneer, and stomp around after a losing effort than to walk over to the guy who just beat you, smile, and offer congratulations. Similarly, after winning, our natural instinct is to gloat over our downhearted opponent.

Just as we had to learn the value of sportsmanship, our kids have to learn it from us. Teaching such a valuable lesson isn't a coach's responsibility—it's a parent's job. That's just as well, since some coaches' idea of sportsmanship is a little sloppy

What Is "Sportsmanship"?

It's often a difficult concept to define to children, but there are some basic parameters that should be taught and reinforced. To be a good sport, you have to:

→ Play by the rules.

→ Be a good loser.

→ Be a gracious winner.

→ Respect the decisions, requests, and opinions of others.

→ Be even-tempered.

→ Respect the abilities and efforts of your opponents.

→ Take turns and let others play.

And in case you didn't notice, "sportsmanship" has nothing to do with winning.

anyway. How many times have you heard a coach say something like:

→ "Hey, ref, what are you—blind? What kind of call was that? You're robbing these kids!"

→ "Hey, don't help him get up! He's on the other team! Let him lie there."

→ "C'mon, Jimmy, don't let that little squirt steal the ball from you! He's half your size!"

In such cases, it's your job as parent to make sure your kid doesn't follow such an example—and to intervene with a coach who doesn't seem to know what sportsmanship is.

TEACH YOUR CHILDREN WELL

Hall of Famer Ernie Banks once said, "If you want to know if you're a good sport, first you have to lose." He's right. Thankfully, plenty of today's top players are good sports and make great role models for your kid. Being able to point out how Grant Hill, Steve Young, or Cal Ripken, Jr. embody sportsmanship is worth a million words on the subject. You can teach kids to respect the athletic ability of a Dennis Rodman or a Charles Barkley, but when it comes to sportsmanship, point out players like Michael Jordan and David Robinson. Explain to them they should try and pattern themselves after players who deserve respect for their actions both on and off the athletic field. As the 1960s song says, "Teach your children well."

Good winners can be proud of themselves without gloating over their opponents.

Some kids get overly nervous, anxious, or even upset before a game, complaining of headaches, stomachaches, invisible illnesses (like back pains, hurt legs, and fever), nausea, or general fatigue. Still others fall prey to excessive moodiness.

In my experience, when a young child feels that upset about playing in a sport, there's some underlying problem he needs—and wants—to talk about. Take a few moments to sit down with your child and gently search for what bothers her about playing.

You might start with, "Honey, I'm a little surprised that you don't want to play softball today. I mean, all your friends will be there, and it's a beautiful day outside. Is there something that happened in practice, or during the last game, that's bothering you?"

Given such an opening, most kids eagerly detail the reasons they're upset, reasons that can be as simple as:

→ a minor misunderstanding between your child and the coach,

→ being teased by a teammate,

→ a general fear of losing,

→ not being able to play a certain position,

→ an overall disappointment in the level of personal play.

Whatever the problem is, once it's out in the open, it's much easier to deal with. Keep a watchful eye for any signs or suggestions that your child isn't having as much fun as she once did. Telltale indications include comments like: "Mom . . . do I have to go to practice today? Can't I stay home and watch TV instead? " or "Don't worry, Dad, it's OK if I'm a little late for the game." Such statements indicate that there's a problem to be brought out into the open.

A WORD ABOUT COMPETITIVE BEHAVIOR—YOURS!

Parents can get caught up in competition as well, so keep an eye on your own behavior. *After all, you're your kid's most important role model.* All of your behavior is being watched carefully by your children—whether you're visibly nervous and cranky before a game, if you use profanity during the competition, yell at the officials, or feel compelled to chastise the coach and lecture your child after the game. Why

Children should be taught to look up to athletes who demonstrate good sportsmanship.

shouldn't a kid assume that this is the "right way" for them to behave? They watched you do it.

Self-discipline is key. Oh, that tough loss may gnaw at you, but you have a responsibility to your children and their friends to say and do the right thing. That means exhibiting good sportsmanship, praising the opposing team's play, shaking hands with sincerity, and giving a pat on the back to the ref or ump for a job well done—even if your child's team lost. In fact, that's the best time to do it. Wait until your kid's asleep to give your pillow an anguished scream.

(*"The younger the kids, the less emphasis on competition."*)

INSIDE TIPS:
→ *Do it the right way:* At the end of a youth league contest, to show good sportsmanlike behavior to your kids, have the parents from opposing teams shake hands out on the field. Then have the parents from either side congratulate the players on the other team. Your kids will quickly get the

 ## Sports Parenting Skills Tip

Parents (and coaches) always want to know if it's dangerous to have their little pitcher learn to throw curve balls. The answer is . . . yes! No youngster should be throwing (or attempt to throw) a curve ball until they're at least fourteen or fifteen years old. The damage that can be done to one's elbow and ulnar nerve is well documented. So please tell your young Nolan Ryan to be patient.

Lots of kids really put their all into the game and can react in an extreme manner whether they win or lose. Sportsmanship takes training and self-discipline.

message that there's more to winning and losing than just the score of the game.

In the fall of 1996, the Green Bay Packers defeated the San Francisco 49ers for the NFC Championship. After the game, Brett Favre, the Green Bay quarterback, was interviewed on national television for his great game. But as Favre was talking on-air with the TV reporter, the great 49ers quarterback Steve Young went up to Brett and said, "Congratulations, Brett, you played a great game. Good luck in the Super Bowl. You deserve all the best." And then Brett thanked Steve for his best wishes.

It was a golden moment in pro sports, because rarely before had a national sports audience seen two great athletes share a sincere moment of honest sportsmanship. It was one of the true

Ken Dryden, goalie for six Montreal Canadien Stanley Cup champion teams, is also a well-respected author and attorney. In his classic book, *The Game*, Dryden writes about the essence of sportsmanship and competition, and how vital it is to respect and honor one's opponent:

> "A good opponent [is] a rare and treasured thing for any team or player. For a good opponent defines a player or a team. By forcing you to be as good as you can be, such an opponent stretches the boundaries of your emotional and playing experience, giving you your highest highs and lowest lows; your best and worst and hardest moments. When you get to an age or to a moment that causes you to look back, you realize how important that is."

In other words, from Dryden's perspective, playing and competing against a worthy opponent is how you learn to stretch your abilities to a higher level. Without that opposing force, you can't go any higher.

highlights of the entire NFL season, because it showed what sports—even at the top levels—was still about: saluting and congratulating one's opponent for a job well done.

→ *Let them all play:* Hey, coach! When it comes to game time, let all the kids play in the game—and make certain that they all get lots of playing time. Think about what the famous Chinese philosopher Lao Tse said, way back in 430 B.C.: "If you tell me, I will listen. If you show me, I will see. If you let me experience it, I will learn."

That philosophy still applies today—especially with kids playing sports. While kids will listen to you when you coach, and they'll watch when their friends play in the game, the only real payoff for kids is to actually play in the game themselves. That's where the fun is—and that's when they'll experience the thrill of the game.

DID YOU KNOW?

Working out with weights is not necessarily a bad thing for kids to do. However—before even thinking about letting your little one run wild in a weight or training/fitness room, check with your pediatrician. Also make certain the attending weight-training instructor is certified in this field.

Kids learn by playing—and they need lots of playing time to improve their skills.

07

BUILDING SELF-ESTEEM THROUGH SPORTS

What do you think retired pro athletes miss most about their playing days? Huge endorsement contracts? Signing bonuses? MVP awards? Slipping on that championship ring?

Nope. Ask one of these retired players what he misses most, and he'll usually say something like, "The guys." That's sports shorthand for the *camaraderie*, the friendships with both teammates and opponents, the goofy clubhouse pranks, and the unwavering emotional support.

It's true. Former players always seem to equate having fun with the friendships and the good times they had, not with statistical achievements and awards like Most Valuable Player, most points scored, or perennial All-Star. It's the personalities, the give-and-take and banter among friends, the solidarity with teammates that they treasure.

What does this say to the parent of a young athlete today? To my mind, the lesson retired pros teach us is that long after the scorebooks are put away, it's the joy of being with one's friends that continues to linger. Sports merely provides a convenient—and fun—vehicle for kids to feel good about themselves, their physical and mental well-being, and their sense of social acceptance. In other words, it's all the components of healthy self-esteem.

WHY KIDS LIKE TO PLAY SPORTS

Now that we've looked at the sporting experience from the other end of the spectrum—the viewpoint of the retired athlete—let's turn it around and go back to the four-year-old. Why are kids drawn to sports at this early age—and what, as a parent, can you do to make certain that your child gets off to a proper start?

According to many child development psychologists, kids as young as two or three exhibit a heightened sense of self-esteem when, after numerous attempts, they

Sports is about friendship and good times.

master a simple athletic task, like kicking a ball or catching one, running quickly from one place to another, or finally tipping over the chair where the cat is sleeping.

If you doubt this, just watch the delight on your four- or five- year-old's face when she swings a bat and makes contact with a ball. Conversely, a young child having trouble hitting the ball will probably end up crying if such frustration continues. But those tears dry up rather quickly once she succeeds in making contact.

(*"Good players rise above bad breaks."*)

This simple (and innate) desire to master a physical skill goes a long way to explaining why kids are so magnetically drawn to electronic games like Sega and Nintendo. Now, the majority of parents might consider the hours kids spend playing these games a waste of time. But such games actually serve a valuable purpose. Kids learn to manipulate the action figures on the TV screen by using, developing, and perfecting eye-and-hand coordination. Game manufacturers realize this attraction to increasing challenge, and build in varying levels of difficulty to keep kids interested. The better kids get at a particular skill, the more challenges they want. And if you really think that such skills are trivial, just try beating your kid at a Sega game some-time.

The same phenomenon happens in sports. Youngsters who develop greater mastery of athletic skills (like running, kicking, and catching) find themselves drawn back to the sport for fresh challenges. Between the ages of four and seven, kids live in a heady world of skill mastery. Every day seems to bring a new challenge and a new success—from walking to riding a bicycle, from simply picking up a ball to throwing and catching one.

It's after this period that a kid begins to understand not just that there are other kids on the planet who have mastered these skills but that there are varying degrees of competence—a pecking order. By the time a kid is seven or eight, it's no longer enough to have learned to ride a two-wheeler, he has to ride it faster than some other kid. But in the early years, ages four to seven, it's enough for your child to gradually master the basic skills of athleticism.

...ng children who master sports skills experience a heightened sense of self-esteem.

Parents are keenly aware of how their kid stacks up against others—usually more so than the kids themselves. At some point, you notice that your five- or six-year-old doesn't seem to be keeping up with his mates. Is this a cause for concern?

Not necessarily. Kids learn and master athletic skills at different speeds. This means not only that an under-sized girl will probably catch up to her peers by the time she's eight or nine, but that your oversized, dominant boy of six will probably fall behind the others as they catch up in size.

You should also recognize —hard as it might be—that chances are, your kid isn't going to be an Olympic champion or top professional athlete. In fact, the over-whelming majority of kids won't even aspire to such lofty athletic goals; that's why it's more important that you help

Self-Esteem in Kids' Sports

Kids do go through a process of self-evaluation in sports, and these evaluations tend to be strongly driven by outside influences, such as their peers, coaches, parents, and others. Reflected appraisal from these sources may be subtle or unintentional (e.g., a smile from the coach or the lack of a smile), but regardless, these have a substantial impact on a youngster's self-evaluation.

Several psychological studies have suggested that when children do not receive the right kinds of reflected appraisal in these situations, that they'll stop taking part in youth sports rather than dealing with their own real or imagined inadequacies.

your child focus on enjoying sports rather than excelling at them. Falling behind her peers isn't a problem if your kid still loves the game, so don't worry if she doesn't make the travel team; she's having fun, and that's what counts.

Now that you have a handle on your kid's development, you have to make sure your kid can deal with it as well. After all, a year in a child's life can bring about HUGE changes.

Consider: Whether you're thirty-seven or thirty-nine or forty-one really doesn't make much of a difference in your athletic ability. Why? Because your athletic and physical size or strength won't vary much on a year-to-year basis.

But a child's entire sporting life can change in one year. A wiry, sure-footed soccer player can suddenly find himself all arms and legs. The shortest girl on the basketball team can go through a growing spurt and find herself the tallest in the game.

PERSONAL EXAMPLE NO. 2

Do changes in age really make a difference? Let me give you an example. When my son, John, was six and playing for the first time in an organized youth league soccer game, his coach put him on defense. Although John had played soccer on a casual basis with his friends in school, he had never played before on a REAL team.

The coach instructed John where to position himself: "Now, this is the spot where you play. If the ball comes to you, kick it back up the field. Got it?" My son dutifully nodded.

Kids between the ages of eight to ten are very concerned with the rules of the game—and what they consider to be fair or unfair.

It wasn't until late in the first half that the ball came John's way; as the ball rolled closer he got ready to deliver a good, hard kick. But instead of kicking it, John watched it roll right by him. It was no more than a foot or two away from him—and inexplicably, he refused to kick it!

At halftime I asked John why he hadn't kicked the ball. He looked me right in the eye and said: "Dad, the coach told me exactly where to stand on the field—and the ball came close to that spot, but not close enough." My six-year-old son had followed his coach's directions perfectly—perhaps a bit too perfectly.

You get the point. Kids at age six are still involved in simply learning the physical basics of sports. It takes a few more years of learning, watching, and playing before their cognitive skills catch up.

And by the way, my son John eventually began to understand that there was a certain amount of latitude in the position you played on the field.

DEALING WITH THE "LAW AND ORDER" PHASE

Something curious happens to kids around the ages eight to ten: they turn into Game Cops. They become downright impassioned and sometimes belligerent over calls that go against their team, and make dramatic pleas for justice:

➔ "But ump, that fly ball wasn't fair. It was foul by a mile!"
➔ "Ref, the ball was out of bounds. It should be our ball!"
➔ "I'm not playing anymore 'cuz the ref is cheating. He's giving all the calls to the other team!"

Kids upset with these seemingly unfair calls are often moved to tears, frustrated that the refs or umps can't—or won't—understand the difference between what's right and what's wrong. Sometimes on the way home after a game, your kid will even ask: "But Mom, why did the ref make such a bad call? And when he realized he was wrong, why didn't he change it?"

This is a good time to introduce an old sports cliché: "Them's the breaks." Referees and umpires are human, and they sometimes make bad calls. Them's the breaks. But the true test of a sportsman is whether he let's such a bad call affect his play. You can point out to your indignant child that good players rise above bad breaks. To a great extent, they even plan for them. How many times have you heard a coach or player explain in a postgame interview: "Sure I disagreed with the call. But bad breaks are part of the game; you can't let them beat you." Your kid has to learn that the key to bad calls—just or unjust—isn't in how you protest them, but how you bounce back from them.

That, ultimately, is the key to success, not only in sports but in life.

Learning new sports skills takes time, effort, and dedication.

WHAT HAPPENED TO THE "DO OVER"?

Before the era of organized youth sports, kids playing in backyards and on sandlots rarely had officials to make rulings. A special sandlot ritual evolved to handle close calls: the "do over." (As in, "OK, we can't decide whether that ball was fair or foul, so let's just do the play again. Let's have a do over.")

The invention of the do over (along with the "invisible runner") was a significant step in social compromise and social interaction. But few kids today, because of the rigid structure in which they play organized sports, know what a do over is.

Feel free to explain the concept of the do over to your own children. It might just help them learn a new way of forging social compromises in sports, just as it helped our generation.

TEARS OF FRUSTRATION = MOTIVATION?

Learning new sports skills always means a challenge. Trying to ice skate, attempting to throw strikes, or trying to dribble a basketball between your legs—all of these advanced skills take time, effort,

Parents can support their children in many ways, whether by sharing their successes and frustrations after a game or by finding a few moments for basketball practice after dinner.

and dedication. Invariably, the most a kid gets out of the first few attempts is hard-core frustration, even tears of frustration.

It's important to focus your kid's efforts on challenges that are reasonable. Asking a young kid to toss a regulation basketball through a hoop ten feet off the ground isn't a reasonable challenge. Most kids won't even get close until they're ten or eleven; it's just too frustrating for younger children. That's why a lot of youth league coaches use hoops no more than six or seven feet off the ground, and basketballs half the size of regulation balls. Kids don't care about the changes. All they know is that they thoroughly enjoy scoring baskets.

The same philosophy applies to baseball. Baseball is a particularly hard game to master because it involves so many skills: hitting, throwing, catching, fielding, and so on. And because of these demanding skills, the game can be particularly daunting for kids under ten. To keep the game challenging but still enjoyable, in some youth leagues a parent or coach handles the pitching chores, or the league uses a pitching machine for both teams. Such a maneuver keeps the game moving quickly, and insures that all the kids can enjoy the game at *their* level of skill. The game is fun, and the kids aren't overwhelmed by the game's complexity.

BE THERE FOR YOUR CHILD

It's important to let your child know that you'll be there no matter what happens—that you're there to celebrate her triumphs, praise her good work, help her work through frustration, talk over her doubts, express your pride, and relive her excitement.

Make it a habit to ask your child about her Big Moments in games of practice.

To find out more about kids and sports, go to www.trainingcamp.com

For kids, the team comes first.

 ## Sports Parenting Skills Tip

When teaching your child how to play basketball, you'll quickly discover that most kids just don't have the physical strength to throw a ball high enough so that it goes into the hoop. You're better off making two adjustments: 1) finding a basketball rim that slides down a pole so that you can adjust it at six or seven feet high, and 2) finding a basketball that is considerably smaller than a regulation-size ball.

You'll discover that children have a lot more fun when they're able to put the ball in the basket, rather than being constantly frustrated by not even coming close.

Remind her how excited and proud you were when she kicked the ball or returned a serve or got up quickly after a tumble. Feel free to embellish the event in the retelling. Nothing builds rapport with a kid more than their knowing your support is always there.

Always bear in mind that a child has only so many years to develop basic skills in sports—usually the years between four and thirteen. That's less than a decade to teach your child some very important things about sports— including sportsmanship, dedication, hard work, goals, practice, and success.

So be clear in your lessons, make them easily understood, and reinforce those key lessons whenever you can.

INSIDE TIPS

➔ *Be sensitive to all the kids:* If you're the head coach of a team, be careful when you single out players for such awards as Most Valuable Player. In most youth league teams, you'll be asked to say a few words about the team at the end of the season. You're always on safe ground if you call each child up individually and praise his efforts for the past season. (This is an extension of Coaching by Walking Around, known as Coaching by Having the Kids Walk Up to You.)

Some coaches, in a well-intentioned gesture, decide to select a team MVP. The price you pay for singling out one thrilled kid as Most Valuable Player might be twenty others who feel bitter, jealous, and confused: "Gee, I thought the Coach thought I was the best player." Be careful handing out MVP or comparable awards; they may hurt a lot more than they help. As one coach pointed out to me, "You stress to the kids all year the importance of team play, of always putting the team first. And then, at the end of the season, you single out only one player? In my mind, there should never be only one team MVP. Every member of that team is a MVP."

➔ *Be creative:* One of the great pleasures of playing with your child is to invent games together. There's no better way to develop skills and self-confidence than by inventing a competition together—especially a competition where the child has the advantage over the grown-up.

In our family, the silly game of "sock throwing" is quite popular. All we do is

When you play basketball or any other sport with your kid, remember to play at their level.

find a wastebasket, put it a few feet away, and then we ball up socks from our drawers and have a quick contest to see who can toss the most socks into the basket.

It's fun and easy to do whether you're six or sixty. There's also no advantage in being older, which allows the kids to take part fully and compete as peers against adults. Try it. It really works!

→ *The real goal:* Here's the truth about your children and youth sports: The real goal is that they enjoyed playing so much, they'll want to play again next year. That's always the real test of whether your child had fun.

08

YOUR KID, THE COACH, AND YOU

Webster's dictionary defines the verb "coach" as: "to train intensively through instruction, demonstration, and practice."

Compare this definition with some of the coaching you've witnessed—or, if you're a coach, with your own method of coaching. From any number of weekend kid's games, you'd think that Webster's had left out the most important parts of coaching: yelling, screaming, and profanity.

Many parents (and their kids) are shocked to discover that the coach of that third-grade team, while as mild-mannered as Dr. Jekyll in daily life, turns into Coach Hyde at game time. But sure enough, there he is, yelling nasty comments to the ref, shouting constant instructions to the children, and sprinkling his loud chatter with a potpourri of curses.

What is it about a game that turns nice, normal people into loud, foul-mouthed jerks? What can parents do about it?

I believe that a lot of adults assume that aggressive, even abusive, coaching methods are what professional coaches use. A lot of adults who coach today model themselves after legendary hard-nosed football coach Vince Lombardi. Mean, tough, and loud, Lombardi was the preeminent coach when most of these adults were kids; it's only natural that they look to him as a role model. But what these grown-ups forget is that Vince Lombardi coached back in the 1960s—and what worked for coaches more than thirty years ago doesn't necessarily work with today's generation of athletes. Very few successful professional or collegiate coaches yell, scream, and shout at their players today. Successful coaches know that, eventually, the players simply tune out such regular abuse, and it's hard to instruct a player who isn't listening anymore.

Want proof? Take a look at today's most successful coaches—like Phil Jackson of the Chicago Bulls, Larry Bird of the Indianapolis Pacers, or Joe Torre of the New York Yankees. Mean, tough, and loud? They rarely even speak, much less raise their

A coach goes over strategy with her Little League team.

voices. And when they do speak, it isn't to yell and scream, but to praise or instruct. That's what works best with today's players.

It's the same for young kids, who just tune out the coach who constantly yells at them during a game. It doesn't matter if the coach is just blowing off steam or if he actually has a valid point to make; his kids just hit the "mute" button as soon as he starts yelling and turn their thoughts to more pleasant things. By trying to communicate forceful-ly, the coach has actually ended communication with his players.

In a recent study conducted and reported by Ronald E. Smith and Frank L. Smoll, these two highly regarded psychologists studied a youth travel soccer team to determine what impact a hard-dri-ven, aggressive coach would have on the team. The study found that the team's formerly so-so record improved dramatically under the aggressive coach.

So hard-nosed coaching does work. But to what end, and for how long? Significantly, several key members of the team didn't show up to play the next season, and one gave up the sport entirely. The reason? The hard-driven coach.

As one player put it: "Yeah, we won, but nobody was really happy. Coach was a total jerk who was mean to everyone and took all the fun out of the game. I'd rather play on a less talented team with a coach and players I like than to go through that again."

Studies such as this should serve as a wake-up call to parents who do worry about their sons and daughters, and the coaches they play for.

Young athletes respond best to coaches who know how to communicate with their players without yelling and swearing.

Does This Stuff Really Happen?

In Cheesequake, New Jersey, three fathers who were coaching in the town's Little League were suspended for two games for arguing calls, using profanity, and challenging each other. The league, by the way, was for six-to-eight-year-olds, where no score or standings were kept.

WHAT ABOUT THE PROFANITY?

Speaking of hard-driven coaches, where is it written that a youth league coach should be free to use obscenities or profanity around young kids?

"Ah, c'mon, kids," I heard one coach say to his young troops. "Sometimes I'll say a bad word during the course of a game. But just ignore it—forget about it. I don't mean it."

What does this say to kids? That there's so much riding on a kids' game it makes a coach lose control of his speech? That swearing is OK, as long as you don't really mean what you're saying? That an effective coaching method is: "Do as I say, not as I do?"

Teachers in classrooms certainly endure more than their share of frustration, and you don't see them swearing. For one thing, parents wouldn't put up with it. But coaches are really just sports teachers, and their classroom is the playing field; they should be held to the same rules of conduct as any other teacher. (This is especially important if, as so often happens, your kid's coach doubles as a school-teacher.)

According to one coach I interviewed: "All these kids have heard worse on the playground at school, or they get this kind of language at home. Everybody does it."

True—a lot of adults use profanity. And many kids—even ones as young as eight or nine—follow their example and use profanity as well.

But there's no reason cursing should be accepted in sports. It certainly isn't tolerated by referees or umpires. In major league baseball, for instance, a

Coaches, like this tennis coach, teach through instruction, demonstration, and drilling.

Parents with special expertise can become coaches, like this father teaching a boy to box. But even if you're not that familiar with a particular sport, you can still help out as an assistant coach.

player can debate a call with an umpire all he wants—but as soon as the player directs one profanity at the ump, he gets tossed. And it's not too much of a jump from swearing and cursing to trash-talking and taunting. There is, of course, no place for that kind of activity in youth sports either.

In some youth programs, the league commissioner actually requires each participating player to sign a letter stipulating that he or she will play according to the rules of sportsmanship. The letter clearly states that profanity and trash-talking are strictly forbidden. Such letters have a great impact on children, especially when their lessons are reinforced by parents. It's just another way of teaching and enforcing sportsmanship.

Finally, remind your kids that cursing and trash-talking doesn't make them into better players; only hard work, talent, and dedication can make them better.

WHEN TO INTERVENE WITH A COACH

It's a rare parent who never wants to have a word with his kid's coach. As any coach is well aware, the list of parental concerns is endless: my kid isn't getting enough quality playing time; he wants to play a different position; she's feeling left out because she has no friends on the team; one of her teammates is teasing her; he comes home in tears because you yell at him.

There's a right way and a wrong way to approach the coach. It's not a great idea to confront him immediately before or after a game, although that might be the most convenient time for you. As for having a private word with a coach during a game, forget it. At best the coach will ignore you in order to do his job. At worst, you and the coach—two of your kid's most important role models—will end up in a nasty argument that defines bad sportsmanship.

$$\left(\textit{``Work with the coach, not against him.''} \right)$$

Rather, find out when it's OK to give the coach a private call at home. (Don't just assume you can give Coach a ring any old time you have a concern. Coaches like to eat, sleep, and relax a little, too.)

When you speak to the coach over the phone, avoid confrontation. Never start out with: "Coach, I got a problem with the way you. . . ." Such an approach immediately puts the coach on the defensive.

Instead, try this approach: "Coach, I was wondering if you could help me with a problem I'm having with my daughter Susie. You see, she's very upset that she's not getting more of a chance at playing on offense. . . ."

Work *with* the coach—not against him. It's my experience that 99 percent of these youth league coaches are much more sympathetic to your concerns if you voice them properly.

One final note about intervening: Some of you might wonder whether you should intervene at all when your kid has a problem. Fearing being seen as pushy and protective, you might conclude that this is a good opportunity for your child to learn to fight his own battles.

Don't make this mistake. If your son or daughter had a problem in school, you'd call the teacher right away to see what was going on. Why shouldn't you do the same with your child's coach? To me, academic education and physical education, especially at the younger ages, should be treated in the same way.

Furthermore, if you stand on the sidelines, metaphorically as well as physically, your child might naturally assume that either you don't care about his athletic pursuits or that the coach is 100 percent correct in his approach. Taking an active role in your child's well-being is only natural.

 To find out more about kids and sports, go to www.trainingcamp.com

Coaches have the chance to become important role models and mentors in the lives of young athletes.

"Kill the Ump!"

It might surprise you to know that *Referee Magazine* routinely includes a section that details assaults and attacks on umpires, referees, and other officials who work Little League and other youth sport games.

In fact, Mel Narol, an attorney based in Princeton, New Jersey, devotes a large amount of his practice to handling the personal injury cases of refs and umps who have been attacked by crazed parents and coaches.

"The best thing about Little League baseball is that it gives the parents something to do on the weekends and keeps them off the streets."

— Bill Geist, *Little League Confidential*

SO WHY AREN'T YOU COACHING?

Good question. Here are some of the typical excuses that parents offer:

→ "Oh, I'm just too busy on the weekends to volunteer to coach."

→ "I'm not that familiar with that particular sport and its rules."

→ "Unfortunately, I'm not that good around little kids." (Hearing this from a parent is always a little disturbing.)

Too little time? I always remind parents that if they really want to share in the joy of their kid's sports lives, there's no better way than by helping out as a coach. But if you don't get involved—well, those precious years go by in a hurry.

Don't know the rules? Ask your kid to explain the game rules to you. Kids love to feel as though they're an authority on the subject. Let her explain soccer's offsides rule, hockey's power play, or pro basketball's illegal defense rule.

Aren't good with kids? You mean you're incapable of watching a bunch of six-year olds have fun? If you're truly uncomfortable around groups of kids, don't be the head coach—be an assistant coach. (Some teams have as many as ten "assistant coaches.")

Best yet, if you help out as an assistant coach, you can make sure the head coach keeps his or her priorities in order. You're that much closer to the action, and can be sure that all the kids get quality playing time, enjoy themselves, and hear lots of praise for their efforts.

INSIDE TIPS

→ Since the vast majority of youth coaches are volunteers, they can use a pat on the back as much as your kid. Don't just give them grief, give them the same encouragement they give your kids. After all, these volunteers are sacrificing their weekends to help coach your kids—so be appreciative of their efforts. Besides, if you think you can do a better job, volunteer yourself.

→ Always take the time to work with your child on his skills. Encourage him to practice on his own. Kids always enjoy it more when their moms and dads work with them; set up little games that they can play and enjoy.

In trying to teach my kids how to kick a soccer ball with either foot, I would simply have them stand about six to eight feet away from me. Then I'd roll a soccer ball to them. Just before the ball was close enough to kick, I'd yell out, "Right!" or "Left!" indicating which foot I wanted them to use to kick the ball back to me.

It's a fun, easy drill to do—and it's one that the kids really enjoy. Try to invent your own games with your kids.

09
SOLO SHOTS:
KIDS WHO CHOOSE INDIVIDUAL SPORTS

Since most kids start out playing team sports for social reasons, many of my comments so far have been about team situations. But if you're the parent of a kid who has a talent for an individual sport—tennis, gymnastics, golf—you probably flipped to this chapter right off the bat, to find out what your kid is in for. What special circumstances surround a child's pursuit of an individual sport? Since many kids actually start playing individual sports at the age of three or four—several years before youth teams become available—the question is an important one.

The psychological pressures that individualized athletes feel can be substantially different from those affecting members of a team. After all, when a child's soccer team wins, he shares the fun and glory of winning with his teammates; and when the team loses, it's nice to be able to divvy up the agony of defeat among the entire squad.

If you're a young tennis player or figure skater, however, the extremes of winning and losing are much more striking. When you win, the glory is all yours, and you get to bask in that beautiful spotlight all by yourself. Conversely, when you lose, it gets pretty lonely in that spotlight, which you wish someone would turn off.

Youngsters quickly grasp this unusual predicament. In response, some learn how to construct alibis for their losses, usually as a means of saving face and protecting their fragile self-esteem. (If some of these alibis sound familiar, remember that some professionals have a hard time dealing with losing, too.) You might hear:

→ "It wasn't fair. The linesman kept calling my shots out when they were in."
→ "I got the worst swimming lane. No wonder I finished third."
→ "The ice surface wasn't smooth enough for me. That's why I couldn't do my best."

Young kids (ages five to nine) usually have a hard time admitting that an opponent was simply better than they were. They're much more comfortable making up excuses for poor performance. As a parent, you have to learn early on how to read your child.

Many young girls start gymnastics at age three or four.

Remember that a postgame analysis is better conducted the day after a game. The only thing to offer right after a game is sincere praise for your kid's effort and a pat on the back for showing a good sense of sportsmanship—whether or not he came out on top. (It's just as hard to be a good winner as a good loser.)

You should address the issue of sportsmanship before your kid ever plays a competitive game. Good sportsmanship is as much a part of any game as its rules and regulations, and has to be learned. You have to make it clear to your child at an early age that regardless of the outcome, it's up to him or her to offer congratulations to opponents immediately after an event.

What if your child refuses? Make it understood, in no uncertain terms, that good sportsmanship isn't an option, but one more rule of play, an essential part of the sport.

Being a bad sport is the same as breaking the rules of play, like using an illegal tennis racket. If your kid refuses to obey the rule of good sportsmanship, he's not respecting the game—and won't be allowed to participate. Despite being momentarily upset, most young kids will toe the line, not wanting to risk being "banned" from the game.

Be forceful about this. This is one of those times when you get to act like a real grown-up parent type and lay down the law to your kid. Enjoy it while it lasts.

Defeat can be difficult for a child to cope with. You shouldn't be too concerned if you see tears of disappointment. This happens with athletes both big and little. A little reassurance that the world isn't about to end, that the sun will rise tomorrow—and, by the way, there's hamburgers for dinner—and within a few minutes your kid will recover. Whatever you do, don't lecture him, embarrass him about crying, or tell him "to act like a grown-up." That not only doesn't accomplish anything but it makes the kid feel even worse about himself. (It also means that you're never allowed to cry, either. Good luck with that!)

If your child won, try to keep the adulation to a moderate level. You can certainly share your child's excitement, but keep it from getting out of control. Most top professional coaches remind their athletes never to allow their emotions to go too high or to drop too low; that's good advice for parents as well. Later in the evening, you can revisit with your child some of the finer points of the competition. As always, get your young athlete (not you) to talk about the parts of the game, and decide whether to continue working on specific skills.

PRACTICING WITH YOUR CHILD

Practice and play with your child as much as possible. There's nothing quite like being able to hit some tennis balls around with your daughter, swim against your son at the local pool, or take a few kids out for a round of golf.

One thing to remember: if your kid wants to compete with you, always make sure you compete in an age-relevant manner. In other words, don't act your age—act your kid's.

A lot of parents protest: "But it doesn't teach children anything if I have to compete at their level. They're better off if they're forced to play against grown-ups—like me."

Think so? How long would you feel like taking batting practice against Randy

Kids who go out for individual sports come to realize that success or failure rests on their shoulders alone.

Johnson throwing at full speed? How much fun would you have playing a game of one-on-one against Karl Malone? A kid who has to play against a grown-up with grown-up abilities quickly realizes that he's never going to win—and eventually loses interest in playing against you. Sometimes, he'll even decide to quit playing the sport altogether. What might have been an invigorating, wonderful time for both you and your kid has

Tiger Woods's Key to Success

By now, you've probably heard how Earl Woods mapped out his son's development in competitive golf while Tiger was still young. But it might surprise you that while Earl, a former Green Beret and strict disciplinarian, had firm ideas about how to teach the sport to his son, it was entirely Tiger's decision whether to play golf at all.

Recalls Tiger: "My Dad never pushed me to play. Whether I practiced or played was always my idea." And what kept Tiger going when he was a kid? "My father always kept the practices fun. It is amazing how much you can learn when you truly enjoy doing something."

The tremendous effort that kids will put into winning a race or a match can make it even harder for them to accept defeat than if they were on a team.

ended with your proving you can beat an eight-year-old. Congratulations.

Go ahead and tell your kid that you'll play tennis against him, but that you'll play the match as if you, too, were eight years old. Your child will like that, because it will make the game that much more enjoyable.

DEALING WITH THE PRESSURE

One of the major differences about participating in an individual sport is that the pressure to win is all on your kid, not spread out among the other members of a team. As any tennis player will tell you, it's a lot harder to shake off a loss when you're the only one losing. Kids who play individual sports—even those as young as seven or eight—need to understand that losing (and winning) reflects one game or performance in a lifetime of games.

It's OK if your child feels rotten after a loss. Silence, pouting, even crying are all okay. Give your child some space to blow off some steam and disappointment. But when you're able, explain that although today wasn't his day, tomorrow might well be. Teach him the old rule that among very talented opponents, on any given day any one of them can emerge victorious. But—and this is the key—just because he didn't win today doesn't mean he's not terrific in his sport or that he won't win tomorrow. After an hour or so, he should start to bounce back.

WILL MY CHILD BECOME THE NEXT SUPERSTAR?

This is a tough question, because it forces you to try and predict the future. If your kid shows some real ability at age four, five, or seven, how do you know whether it's worth the time, effort, and financial and emotional expense to let him or her pursue that talent?

In certain sports, an athlete reaches his peak as a teenager. We know from watching the Olympic games that most of the world's top swimmers record their best times when they are nineteen or twenty. The best gymnasts go for the gold at sixteen or seventeen. Tara Lipinski won the 1997 national figure skating championship at the

It can be very difficult to tell whether a really talented young athlete will continue to improve into his teenage years and beyond.

advanced age of fourteen, and sixteen-year-old Martina Hingis became the world's top-ranked female tennis player.

And let's not forget Tiger Woods, taking the world of golf by storm at the relatively tender age of twenty-one.

With all this headline evidence that kids are blossoming at younger ages, how can you tell whether your child is going to be one of the chosen ones?

IS YOUR CHILD THE GOLDEN ONE?

Time for a reality check. As a parent, you're the last person to be able to objectively assess your kid's talent. If you suspect that your child might be truly exceptional in a sport, before you yank her out of elementary school to have her train and compete full time, before you get that second mortgage to pay off her travel and coaching expenses, before you contact a big-time sports agent to handle the inevitable endorsement contracts, have at least three top coaches evaluate your kid. (Ideally, these three top coaches should have no emotional attachment to your son or daughter.)

That's not all. In addition to these three coaches' evaluation of your child's cur-

 ## Sports Parenting Skills Tip

Swimming is not just fun. It is often a matter of life or death, and should be considered an essential part of anyone's education. Because few of us can learn to float, let alone actually swim, on our own, it's well worth the time and effort to have your youngster sign up for swimming lessons at your local YMCA or town recreational department.

Swimming is one of those sports that yield a lifetime of enjoyment.

rent abilities, it's also important to obtain their evaluation of your child's projected abilities. It's nice to have professional confirmation that your kid is talented now, but—more importantly—you need some sense of how good these experts think your child will be in a few years' time.

Example: Your nine-year-old is exceptionally big and burly for his size. The velocity of his serve blows away his opponents, and he has terrific power with his strokes. You start dreaming of Wimbledon.

But a smart tennis coach might have a different take. That coach, seeing a kid who is certainly talented for his age bracket and plays with power, realizes that both parents are relatively short, stout, and non-athletic, as is the kid's fifteen-year-old older sister. The coach could reasonably conclude that by the time your kid is a teenager, he'll be short and stocky for his size—and an unlikely candidate for Wimbledon. The coach would be wise to gently discourage your nine-year-old's single-minded pursuit of tennis.

$$\left(\text{\textit{"It's just as hard to be a good winner as a good loser."}} \right)$$

On the other hand, perhaps the various coaches you contact are unanimous in their appraisal of your child's abilities: your kid does have a shot at the big time. If that's the case, then you have to discuss the potential changes in lifestyle with your child, the coach, and most importantly, with your spouse. This is a very tricky decision to make, one that requires serious consideration and delicate handling. Don't make it lightly.

Why the concern? Deciding to let your child pursue that singular goal in gymnastics, tennis, or figure skating not only opens the door to a professional career for your kid but it also closes the door on a traditional childhood. Sports—not school, not friends, not family—is going to be your kid's top priority. From here on out, everything—including your own life—will revolve around your kid's pursuit of sport. Out go regular school hours; tutors will help him keep up. Gone are the days of just hanging out with friends his own age; instead he'll spend most of his time with adult coaches. As for romance—well, a life spent practicing, competing, and being exhausted from

To find out more about kids and sports, go to www.trainingcamp.com

Your child's coach can be one of the best judges of her chances at future success in sports.

both is hardly conducive to that.

At the same time, you'll know that for every thousand talented kids chasing this high-powered dream, only two or three are ever going to see their dreams come true. The rest will have memories of their pursuit, but most will eventually drift back to their hometowns, happy that they gave this dream their best shot—but very much aware that they sacrificed their childhood for it.

What if your child is excellent in an individualized sport, but you don't want to throw your entire family's life behind the single-minded pursuit of a dream? Does that mean abandoning any hope that your kid might be a professional some day? Does it mean all that talent is "going to waste?"

Of course not. As one parent explained: "Look, I think it's great that Craig has such a great interest in tennis at an early age. But all we care about is that he enjoys it. Of course, if he really does excel at it, well, maybe he'll play in college, too."

Craig's parents weren't hoping that with his talent Craig might one day turn professional. All they wanted was for Craig to keep having fun playing tennis. Such a level-headed attitude is quite refreshing. Craig's parents realized that by the time he turned thirteen or fourteen, if he were an outstanding tennis player, it would be apparent not only to his own family but to other tennis enthusiasts in the area. Tennis coaches would find their way to his door, and at that point Craig and his family could decide what their next goals in tennis would be.

That makes a lot more sense to me than trying to gamble on a young athlete who isn't yet ten years old, with a long way to go in terms of physical and emotional development. But again, I realize this is still a personal decision for every family. All I'm attempting to do here is point out both the upsides and downsides of the situation.

DID YOU KNOW?

By the time boys reach the age of twelve, they have reached 84 percent of their full adult height. Girls, by the time they're twelve, have reached 93 percent of their full height.

What About Those Who Don't Make It?

For every Tiger Woods or Martina Hingis, sadly, there are thousands of other young talented athletes you've probably never heard of. Like Beverly Klass.

When Beverly was nine, she was such an extraordinary young golfer that she was playing on the LPGA tour. Although only a fourth-grader, she could drive a ball well over 200 yards. Impressed by her potential, her father pushed her so hard to practice and compete that by the time Beverly was thirteen, she had all but had enough of playing golf.

Nevertheless, her father kept pushing her to perform. Within a year, Beverly ran away from home—and remained on the lam for close to two years. Eventually, she was able to return home and receive some counseling. Now forty, Beverly works as a teaching pro at a Florida club, but one can only wonder how different her golfing career might have been if her father hadn't pushed her at such a young age.

Even if your kid is not destined for future stardom, mastering individual sports can give him countless hours of challenge and fun.

SPORTS AND TEENAGERS

No matter how athletically gifted your youngster may be during elementary school, all that can change drastically when he becomes a teenager. A chunky kid slims down. A girl once very tall for her age sees her growth taper off, while everyone else in her class catches up to her. Slow-running kids become fast kids. Short kids suddenly start towering over their parents. And the emotional changes that accompany adolescence, although no less exhilarating or terrifying, are much more subtle.

Such natural changes can have a tremendous impact on your child's relationship to sports. It doesn't just *feel* like a whole new ball game—in many cases that's exactly what it is.

For the most part, how your child enjoyed his formative years will determine whether he'll want to continue playing and competing at higher levels. For some kids, continuing to play sports is only natural; it's something they enjoy and look forward to.

For others, playing at the junior high level or high school level is problematic. For example, your kid might walk into the house one day and say: "You know, Mom, I like playing basketball with my friends, but I don't know about playing the game full time on the school team."

You might find this hard to believe. As far as you're concerned, high school is precisely when a talented kid should come into her own as an athlete. The glory years! Why would she want to stop playing *now?*

Try looking at the question from your teenager's point of view. As an adolescent, whole new vistas are opening up: extracurricular clubs, part-time jobs, learning to drive, dating, even the demands of more schoolwork. It's only natural that such new, exciting opportunities draw her attention away from something she's been doing for years.

This is when you should take a deep breath, forget about how much you've invested in your kid's athletic career, and have a serious talk with your teenage son or daughter. Find out whether she wants to continue to play sports on the more

competitive school teams, or only on the local recreational squads, or perhaps just play for fun with friends and families.

Notice that none of the above options is "forget about exercise entirely." The question isn't whether your kid is going to exercise at all, but what form that exercise will take. You should make it clear that you feel strongly about physical fitness—that some form of exercise is necessary just to keep a body strong. But once that's understood, the decision as to what kind of sports to play is in your kid's hands. You can certainly question him about his reasons for giving up a sport, point out how good he is at his sport, remind him how much fun he had in the past, and reiterate the various benefits of continuing to play—but in the end, it's your kid's choice.

When your kid becomes an adolescent, everything changes—her body, her mind, and quite possibly, her choice in sports.

Of course not. Is there ever such a thing as a "final word" with a teenager? Some kids find that spending a season away from a sport recharges their sports batteries, and they come back even more strongly the following season. Realizing how much they miss playing, they return with an even greater appreciation of competition, camaraderie, and the simple joy of sport.

> **"High school should be the pinnacle, but not the end, of a kid's love affair with sports."**

If that happens, it's great. This is one of those rare times when you get to just stand by and applaud your kid's decision—and of course, remind him that he'll have to work hard in the off-season to catch up with those friends who did play last season. Teenagers are forever changing their minds—it's one of the perks of adolescence. You're there to provide mature and gentle guidance, to show the pros and cons of their decisions.

WHAT MOTIVATES TEENAGERS TO PRACTICE?

This goes back to that vital first component of success—*passion*. Without that unbridled enthusiasm for the game, no amount of pushing or prodding will get teenagers to practice on their own. If, on the other hand, your child really enjoys spending endless hour after hour shooting baskets, dribbling a soccer ball, or swimming laps, rest assured that your child has really connected with the sport. There's no need for you to remind them to do something when they're doing it on their own.

For many kids, however, practice isn't a pleasure; it's a chore. And as such, they tend to lose sight of the reason why they are playing sports in the first place: because it's supposed to be fun.

Teenagers—like grown-ups—should never give up exercise entirely.
But the exercise they choose does not have to be organized sports.

Indeed, many high school coaches complain that it's hard to get enough top athletes to go out for varsity teams these days. "One kid tells me he'd rather work in a convenience store, where he can make some extra cash to buy a car, than spend five days a week practicing," a coach told me. "And another kid says that since he's not going to get enough playing time as a sophomore, he'll do something else this winter, and then come back next season when he can play more."

I believe that this is the result of putting kids under pressure at too early an age. High school should be the pinnacle, not the end, of a kid's sporting career.

One talented athlete told me recently, "Y'know, I was always taught that if you're gonna compete, you might as well be the best. Well, it's clear that I'm not going to be the star on this high school team, so why bother making the effort? I'd be better off getting a job after school."

I pointed out to the boy that he's going to be working for the rest of his life, but he's only got four years to play high school sports. Furthermore, since he was already in tenth grade, he had only two more years ahead of him as an athlete. Unfortunately, none

"Your Son Is Big for His Age"

The next time somebody remarks about how large your son has grown, keep in mind that slugger Cecil Fielder's son, Prince, measures five-foot-nine-inches tall and weighs more than 200 pounds. Not too bad for a boy who, when he was twelve-years-old, routinely took batting practise with the Yankees and hit homers over the wall in spring training.

"He's way more advanced than I was," notes Papa Fielder. "I wasn't even playing baseball at his age." Cecil played primarily basketball as a youngster, switching to baseball when he was in his mid-teens.

of that mattered to him. If he wasn't going to be a star, he didn't see any point in playing. But what about the fun? I asked. His reply: "It would only be fun if I were the star . . . and since that isn't going to happen . . ."

KEEPING THE GAME FUN

Teenagers can be quite unpredictable, as you probably know; consistency isn't their strong suit. Still, if sports have always been an outlet for fun in your kid's life, there's no reason for her to abandon it as a teenager—unless it stops being fun, that is.

One of the reasons participating stops being fun is competition. Teenagers are much more aware of how they stack up against their peers than they were as youngsters—whether the subject is academic achievement, popularity, or athletic prowess. It's in early adolescence, as they compete with one another for spots on a junior high school team roster, that these twelve- or thirteen-year-olds first come face-to-face with the hard edge of competition. And since there are more ordinary players than outstanding ones, most kids feel like they're falling short of the mark.

At the same time, the effectiveness of parental praise seems to diminish. You attempt to bolster your kid's spirit with a little heartfelt praise, and what happens? Your son or daughter either ignores you, nods in dismissal, or says something like, "Oh, c'mon, Mom, I stunk out there . . . and the coach knows it, too!"

Having your kid discount your sincere praise is always vexing. What can you do to inspire your kid? I've found that a little outside intervention works

By the time kids like these are in junior high school, they know how they stack up against their peers.

wonders; get an adult outside the family to speak with your kid—ideally, a neighbor or family friend. If your comments don't count because you're a parent, an outsider's comments can mean a lot to your kid.

Example: "Say, Jessie, I had a chance the other day to watch you perform. Wow! I had heard you were good, but you were down-right terrific!"

Jessie: "Gee, thanks, Mr. Monroe. I had no idea you were at the game."

Mr. Monroe: "I sure was . . . and I gotta tell you, you played great!"

Kids who dismiss family praise as biased almost always respond to praise from someone outside the immediate family. After all, by now teenagers naturally assume that parents have to say nice things to them about their abilities—that's part of the Parental Oath. But praise from an impartial outsider is gold to a teenager who may doubt his ability.

The good thing about sports today is that even if your child stops playing competitive sports, there are lots of other recreational sports to choose from. Parasailing, anyone?

DID YOU KNOW?

Only one in 10,000 high school basketball players makes it to the NBA. Yet despite these odds, the love of the sport—not some imaginary future stardom—keeps kids playing the game.

Keep in mind that it's your kid's sense of self-esteem, not some objective standard of play, that determines whether he wants to go on playing. If he feels that he's a good player—not necessarily a great player, or a star, or the best on the team—and he enjoys the competition, why should he ever give up playing? A pat on the back at the right time can do wonders for him—even if someone else has to do the patting.

Sadly, there may come a time when your kid realizes that he can't be as competitive as he wishes, and as a result, decides to stop playing. This is always a difficult time for child and parent, and unfortunately it happens all too often and at too early an age. The growing demands of competition can overwhelm your kid's desire to keep on playing "just for fun."

If this happens, help him understand that he can continue to enjoy the sporting scene; there are lots of other recreational sports and activities still to choose from.

Adolescence and Athletic Ability

One of the few long-range studies on kids and athletics shows how much change children go through as they mature. The Medford growth study took a twelve-year longitudinal view of kids and youth sports. The study found that from the time the children started playing sports in elementary school to the time they were ready for high school, only one out of four top-rated athletes who had been rated as a "star" athlete in the youth leagues was still considered a "star."

A FINAL CHECKLIST FOR ALL PARENTS

Raising a child—particularly a child who aspires to be an athlete—is hardly an easy task. The road from their very first game to playing sports in junior high is an emotional roller coaster—full of twists, turns, highs, lows, decisions, occasional setbacks, lots of smiles and high-fives.

I've written this book to help you keep everything in perspective during such a wild ride, to point out important milestones in your child's sports career, to alert you to some of the pitfalls that await, and to answer some of your most common questions.

As a final aid, here are some questions to bear in mind. There is no scoring, but I do ask that you be honest and thoughtful in your answers. If you find that some of your answers trouble you, then simply go back to some of the key steps that are outlined in this book.

➔   Have you allowed your kids to chase their dreams in sports?
➔   Have you let your children enjoy themselves while playing?
➔   Do you openly encourage your kids and praise them sincerely for their efforts?
➔   Does your child know how to act like a good sport, regardless of the outcome of the game?
➔   Does your child understand that frustration is part of playing sports and that for every winner, there's also a loser? Do you understand that concept yourself?
➔   Do you and your child understand that physical fitness is important not just for youth sports but also for one's survival in life and general well-being?
➔   Do you have the courage to intervene on behalf of your child if you honestly feel the wrong lessons are being taught by a coach or instructor?
➔   Do you fully understand that your own behavior is a template for your child's behavior?
➔   Does your child know how proud you are of him and his efforts?

Above all, remember this: it's supposed to be about having *fun*. That is—and will continue to be—the ultimate priority in youth sports. And if you can see pure glee and laughter on your child's face as he plays, then you already know how wonderful this entire experience can be.

To find out more about kids and sports, go to www.trainingcamp.com

Having fun and being with friends—that's what youth sports is all about.

For more information about The Training Camp, visit our website at www.trainingcamp.com or call us at 1-800-ATHLETE.

NOTES

Page 13. "Did You Know?": *New York Times* (April 26, 1992). **Page 32.** "Learn From the Pros": Grant Hill, *Change the Game* (NY: Warner, 1996). Page 33. "Did You Know?": Terry Orlick and Cal Botterill, *Every Kid Can Win* (Chicago: Nelson-Hall, Inc., 1975). **Page 38.** "Should a Child Specialize in Just One Sport?": David Hemery, *The Pursuit of Sporting Excellence* (Champaign, IL: Human Kinetics Publishing, 1988). **Page 43.** "Did You Know?": *Consumer Products Safety Commission Report*, 1997. **Page 49.** "Wash Out Syndrome": McPherson, Guppy, and McKay, 1976; Devereaux, 1976; Orlick, 1973; Orlick and Botterill, 1975; Klint and Weiss, 1986—all in Stephen Figler and Gail Whitaker, eds., *Sport and Play in American Life* (Dubuque, IO: William Brown, Inc., 1991). **Page 52.** "This Too Shall Pass": Rick Wolff, *Good Sports* (Champaign, IL: Sagamore, 1997). Page 60. "Do the Pros Let Their Kids Play?": Rainer Martens, Ph.D., *Joy and Sadness in Children's Sports* (Champaign, IL: Human Kinetics Publishing, 1978), 54. **Page 60.** "Did You Know?": Consumer Products Safety Commission Report, (1997). **Page 66.** "What Is 'Sportsmanship?' ": *Joy and Sadness in Children's Sports*, 270. **Page 72.** "Why Respecting One's Opponent Is Key": Ken Dryden, *The Game* (NY: Penguin, 1984). **Page 72.** "Did You Know?": William Kraemer, Ph.D. and Steven Fleck, Ph.D., *Strength Training for Athletes* (Champaign, IL: Human Kinetics Publishing, 1993). **Page 78.** "Self-Esteem in Kids' Sports": Zajonc, 1965; Smith and Smoll, 1982; Horn, 1985; Scanlan, 1978—all in *Sport and Play in American Life.* **Page 85.** "Did You Know?": American Youth Soccer Organization. **Page 88.** Ronald E. Smith and Frank L. Smoll, "Coach-Mediated Team Building in Youth Sports," *The Journal of Applied Sport Psychology* (March 1997), 114-132. **Page 90.** "Does This Stuff Really Happen?": *New York Post* (May 22, 1991). **Page 96.** "Observation": Bill Geist, *Little League Confidential* (NY: Macmillan, 1992). **Page 102.** "Tiger Woods's Key to Success": Earl Woods and Pete McDaniel, *Training a Tiger* (NY: HarperCollins, 1997). **Page 108.** "Did You Know?": William Kraemer, Ph.D. and Steven Fleck, Ph.D., *Strength Training for Athletes* (Champaign, IL: Human Kinetics Publishing, 1993), 11. **Page 109.** "What About Those Who Don't Make It?": *New York Times* (April 8, 1997). **Page 115.** " 'Your Son Is Big for His Age' ": *New York Times*, (March 25, 1997.) Page 177. "Adolescence and Athletic Ability": H.H. Clarke, "Characteristics of Young Athletes," *Kinesiology Review* (1968), 33-42.